THE STORY OF
THE BIBLE

VOLUME I
THE OLD TESTAMENT

TEST BOOK

Cataloging-in-Publication data on file with the Library of Congress.

Illustrations by Chris Pelicano

ISBN: 978-1-61890-664-9

Printed and bound in the United States of America

TAN Books
www.TANBooks.com
Charlotte, North Carolina
2015

THE STORY OF
THE BIBLE

VOLUME I
THE OLD TESTAMENT

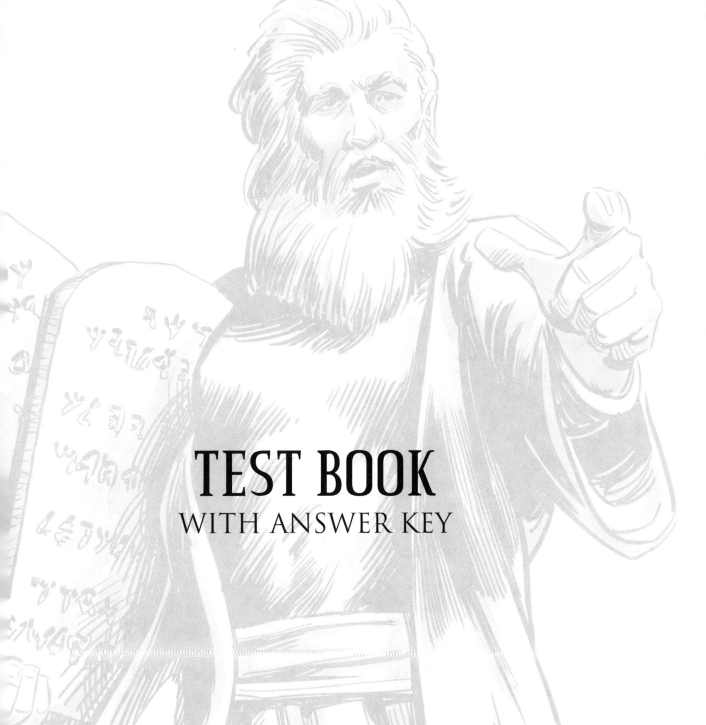

TEST BOOK
WITH ANSWER KEY

CONTENTS

A Word to the Teacher 9

Introduction: Your Time Has Come 11

PART ONE: How God Came to Promise Us a Redeemer

Chapter 1: In the Beginning 15

Chapter 2: The Descendants of Adam and Eve 19

PART TWO: How God Founded the Nation From Which the Redeemer of the World Came

Chapter 3: Abraham and Isaac 23

Chapter 4: Jacob, the Son of Isaac 27

Chapter 5: Joseph, the Son of Jacob 31

PART THREE: How God Protected His Chosen People and Led Them Into the Promised Land

Chapter 6: God Calls Moses to Lead His People 35

Chapter 7: The Escape From Egypt 39

Chapter 8: The Revelation of God's Law 43

Chapter 9: The Desert Wanderings of the Israelites 47

Chapter 10: Joshua, Commander of the Israelites 51

Chapter 11: The Israelites in the Promised Land 55

PART FOUR: How God's Chosen People Lived Under Their Kings

Chapter 12: Saul and David 59

Chapter 13: David's Reign 63

Chapter 14: The Israelites Under King Solomon 67

Chapter 15: Jeroboam and Rehoboam 71

Chapter 16: Elijah the Prophet 75

Chapter 17: The Stories of Job and Jonah 79

PART FIVE: How God's People Went Into Exile and Returned

Chapter 18: The Assyrian Invasions 83

Chapter 19: Daniel and the Babylonian Captivity 87

Chapter 20: The Prophets 91

Chapter 21: The Return to Jerusalem 95

Chapter 22: The Last Days of the Kingdom of Judah 99

Answer Key 103

O sing to the Lord a new song,
for he has done marvelous things!
His right hand and his holy arm
    have gotten him victory.

The Lord has made known his victory,
    he has revealed his vindication in the sight of the nations.

He has remembered his steadfast love and faithfulness
    to the house of Israel.

—Psalm 98 (1–3a)

THE OLD TESTAMENT

A Word to the Teacher

More than eighty years have passed since the publication of *Bible History: A Textbook of the Old and New Testaments for Catholic Schools* (1931). The book soon became a standard text in Catholic schools, for students in the grades we would now call middle school. Since that time, *Bible History* has become a popular text for Catholic homeschooled students.

The time has now come for an updated version that is more complete and more accessible to contemporary readers. The new and expanded version of the textbook, published by TAN Books as *The Story of the Bible*, appears in two volumes: Volume 1, *The Old Testament*, and Volume 2, *The New Testament*. Vocabulary, style, and historical and geographical references have been updated; the text features a new design with fresh illustrations; and some of the material has been reorganized for a clearer presentation.

Most significantly, the New Testament history, which previously focused on the Gospels and concluded with the events reported in Acts 2, now includes six additional chapters. These final chapters tell about the last decades of the biblical story as the newborn Church grew rapidly and began to suffer persecution. They take readers through the remainder of the Book of Acts, focusing—as that book does—on the ministries of the Apostles Peter and Paul. The last chapter concludes with brief remarks about how the New Testament epistles and the Book of Revelation, though not themselves historical narratives, nevertheless contribute to our historical knowledge of the earliest Christians.

Enhanced Storytelling
The new title, *The Story of the Bible*, reflects a new emphasis in presentation on the narrative aspect of the biblical text. Young people love a good story, and Scripture is full of good

stories: in the Old Testament, from the poetic description of creation to the high dramas of prophets, kings, and conquerors; in the New Testament, from the compelling parables of Our Lord to the startling visions of the Apocalypse.

The storytelling aspect of the two new volumes has been especially enhanced in two ways. First, the dynamic style of the new illustrations contributes powerfully to the narrative. Second, an audio recording of the texts is now available so that students can enjoy the biblical stories, not just as readers, but also as listeners. The recording also makes it possible for younger students to enjoy the texts before they have acquired the reading vocabulary required for the books.

Using the Test Book

The revisions of the textbook were extensive enough to require a completely new test book. Like the previous test book, this one provides questions for each chapter that are suitable as a study exercise or as an objective answer test, with an answer key at the end. But the questions now include not only matching items, but multiple choice items as well (along with a few true/false), rather than fill-in-the-blank. Questions for Volume 1 of the textbook are included in this new test book.

Teachers should note that when Scripture is quoted in *The Story of the Bible*, the translation now used in the Old Testament volume is the Revised Standard Version, 2nd Catholic Edition. For this reason, the spelling of the names of people and places will reflect more contemporary usage, rather than the spellings in the older Douay-Rheims translation.

Finally, we should note that supplementary materials for use with the textbook and this test book are available for free download at the publisher's website: www.TANBooks.com.

St. Jerome, an ancient Doctor of the Church and Bible translator known as "the father of biblical scholarship," once said: "Ignorance of Scripture is ignorance of Christ." Our prayer is that *The Story of the Bible* and the accompanying test books will tell the story of Scripture in such a way that young readers will be drawn closer to Our Lord, who is Himself the eternal Word of God.

The Editors

INTRODUCTION
Your Time Has Come

Textbook pages: 7–12
Perfect score: 100

Your Score: _____

Multiple Choice

Directions: For each numbered item, circle the letter beside the choice (A, B, C, or D) that best answers the question or completes the statement. Circle only one choice per item. Each correct answer is worth 4 points. 60 possible points.

1. We can learn about God from:

A. the natural beauty and power of the things He has created.
B. the love of the people who care for us.
C. the Bible.
D. all of the above.

2. Which of the following does *not* demonstrate why the "Book of Nature" only partially teaches us all we need to know about God?

A. Sometimes we read the wonderful lessons found in the "Book of Nature" incorrectly.
B. The things of this world are so beautiful and powerful and good that we may be tempted to think more of them than we do of the God who made them.
C. The "Book of Nature" cannot be understood even in a limited way.
D. Many important things about God and His will for us are above and beyond nature.

3. A truth that is above and beyond nature is called:

A. natural.
B. preternatural.
C. unnatural.
D. supernatural.

4. The truths that we can't fully understand, even after God has told them to us, we call:

A. mysteries.
B. fables.
C. half-truths.
D. myths.

5. God gave the sacred writers who wrote the Bible a special kind of help that He has given to no other writers; we call this unique kind of assistance:

A. literary elegance.
B. clarity of speech.
C. divine inspiration.
D. natural law.

6. The Church cannot make a mistake when she tells us what we must believe and do if we wish to know, love, and serve God, both in this life and the next. In these matters, the Church is:

A. fallible.
B. infallible.
C. generally reliable.
D. uncertain.

7. The Bible is divided into two parts:

A. the Law and the Prophets.
B. the Old Testament and the New Testament.
C. the Gospel and the Epistles.
D. the Psalms and the Chronicles.

8. In the Bible, the word "testament" means:

A. a contract.
B. a commercial transaction.
C. a story.
D. a covenant.

9. The Old Testament tells us about:

A. the life of Jesus and His mother.
B. the history of the early Church in Jerusalem.
C. the history of all the nations in ancient times.
D. the covenant between God and His people before Jesus came into the world.

10. The New Testament tells us about:

A. how God's promise was fulfilled in Jesus Christ and His Church.
B. the history of the ancient Israelites.
C. the history of the Church in the Middle Ages.
D. the history of all the nations in modern times.

11. The primary purpose of the moral books in the Old Testament is to:

A. provide historical information about past events.
B. offer rules of conduct for how to live properly.
C. foretell things that will happen in the future.
D. entertain with interesting stories.

12. Another name for the Bible is:

A. Sacred Liturgy.
B. Sacred Scripture.
C. Lectio Divina.
D. Sacred Tradition.

13. Truths about our faith that were not written down in the Bible, but have come to us by word of mouth and by example, beginning with the apostles, are known as:

A. Sacred Liturgy.
B. Sacred Scripture.
C. Lectio Divina.
D. Sacred Tradition.

14. How many books does the Old Testament contain?

A. 29
B. 58
C. 46
D. 66

15. How many books does the New Testament contain?

A. 27
B. 58
C. 45
D. 66

Old Testament or New?

Directions: The following books are from the Bible. Write "OT" in the blank beside the name of a book if it appears in the Old Testament; write "NT" in the blank beside the name of a book if it appears in the New Testament. Note that the books of the Bible are usually called by the main word in their title. For example, *The Gospel According to St. Luke* is called *Luke.* Each blank is worth 2 points. 40 possible points.

1. _____ Revelation

2. _____ Romans

3. _____ Deuteronomy

4. _____ Matthew

5. _____ Sirach

6. _____ Luke

7. _____ Isaiah

8. _____ Jeremiah

9. _____ 1 and 2 Maccabees

10. _____ Genesis

11. _____ Daniel

12. _____ Psalms

13. _____ John

14. _____ Jude

15. _____ 1 and 2 Corinthians

16. _____ Judith

17. _____ Exodus

18. _____ Acts of the Apostles

19. _____ Leviticus

20. _____ Zechariah

PART ONE
How God Came to Promise Us a Redeemer

CHAPTER 1
In the Beginning

Textbook pages: 13–24
Perfect score: 100

Your Score: _____

True or False?

Directions: In the blank beside each statement, write "T" if the statement is true, or "F" if the statement is false. Each correct answer is worth 3 points. 30 possible points.

_____ 1. Like everything else, God had a beginning and will have an end.

_____ 2. God can enter our world, while still remaining outside of time.

_____ 3. God is infinitely perfect; He needs nothing.

_____ 4. Among the three Divine Persons, the Father and the Son are equal to each other, but the Holy Spirit is not equal to them.

_____ 5. God made the human race because He was lonely.

_____ 6. God knows all things.

_____ 7. God created heaven and earth out of nothing.

_____ 8. God wants His creatures to share in His happiness and glory.

_____ 9. The word "day," as used in the Bible, always means a period of twenty-four hours.

_____ 10. The first book of the Bible is Matthew.

Matching

Directions: In each blank beside a phrase, write the letter of the term that is described by that phrase. Each item is worth 2 points. 14 possible points.

A. intellect   E. Michael
B. free will   F. original sin
C. choirs   G. Lucifer
D. demons

_____ 1. the fallen angels

_____ 2. the first sin of Adam and Eve

_____ 3. leader of the rebel angels

_____ 4. the ability to think

_____ 5. leader of the good angels who fought the bad angels

_____ 6. the nine ranks of angelic spirits

_____ 7. the ability to choose

Multiple Choice

Directions: For each numbered item, circle the letter beside the choice (A, B, C, or D) that best answers the question or completes the statement. Circle only one choice per item. Each correct answer is worth 4 points. 56 possible points.

1. In the first creation story of the Book of Genesis, which of the following is created last by God?

A. light
B. human beings
C. the fish, birds, and other animals
D. the earth and seas

2. The seventh day, on which God rested, was called:

A. a holiday.
B. a work day.
C. a day of penance.
D. the Sabbath.

3. According to Genesis, which creature was created by God in His own image and likeness?

A. the angels
B. the cherubim
C. human beings
D. the seraphim

4. The name *Adam* means:

A. from the ground.
B. the man.
C. father of all living.
D. either A or B above.

5. The name *Eve* means:

A. mother of all living
B. the woman.
C. from the sea.
D. either A or B above.

6. God said that Adam and Eve could eat the fruit from any tree in the Garden of Eden except:

A. the tree of life.
B. the tree of the knowledge of good and evil.
C. the tree of death.
D. the tree of righteousness.

7. Satan appeared to Eve in the form of:

A. a serpent.
B. a good angel.
C. a man.
D. a woman.

8. The serpent tempted and deceived Eve by telling her that:

A. if she ate the fruit, nothing would happen to her.
B. all the trees in the garden had the same fruit.
C. God had not told her the truth.
D. God actually wanted her to eat the fruit.

9. Good created Adam and Eve with a right ordering called:

A. original perseverance.
B. original fruitfulness.
C. original righteousness.
D. original prudence.

10. The only human beings never stained by original sin were:

A. St. Joseph and the Blessed Virgin Mary.
B. Jesus Christ and the apostles.
C. Jesus Christ and the Blessed Virgin Mary.
D. Jesus Christ and the prophets.

11. When Adam and Eve realized what they had done, how did they respond?

A. Adam blamed Eve.
B. Eve blamed the serpent.
C. Adam and Eve tried to hide from God.
D. All of the above.

12. God's words, "You are dust, and to dust you shall return," meant that:

A. after death, the bodies of Adam and Eve would go back to the soil from which they were made.
B. Adam would have to farm the soil to grow food.
C. the serpent would crawl on his belly in the dirt.
D. Eve would have to gather wild plants from the ground for food.

13. After God cast Adam and Eve out of the Garden of Eden, they never returned because:

A. they couldn't find their way back to it.
B. they didn't want to live there anymore.
C. God stationed angels with a flaming sword to keep them out.
D. they found a better place to live.

14. All generations of the human race since Adam and Eve lack original righteousness because:

A. they imitate their ancestors' sin.
B. Adam and Eve couldn't pass on what they themselves no longer possessed.
C. the serpent keeps tricking them.
D. they can't locate the Garden of Eden.

CHAPTER 2
The Descendants of Adam and Eve

Textbook pages: 25–34
Perfect score: 100

Your Score: _____

Matching

Directions: In each blank beside a phrase, write the letter of the term that is described by that phrase. You may match more than one description to a single term. Each item is worth 3 points. 60 possible points.

A. Cain   C. Ham   E. Babel   G. Canaan   I. Euphrates
B. Abel   D. Noah   F. Mesopotamia   H. Egypt

_____ 1. the land where God's chosen people eventually came to settle

_____ 2. the land of the Nile River

_____ 3. received a mark from God

_____ 4. God was displeased with his sacrifice

_____ 5. one of Noah's sons

_____ 6. "the land between the rivers"

_____ 7. sent out a raven

_____ 8. murdered his brother

_____ 9. worked as a shepherd

_____ 10. means "confusion"

_____ 11. wandered the earth as an exile

_____ 12. offered a sacrifice to God after the great flood was over

_____ 13. a giant tower never completed

_____ 14. worked as a farmer

question continued on next page ➡

_____ 15. made fun of his father

_____ 16. city where the people were scattered by God

_____ 17. asked, "Am I my brother's keeper?"

_____ 18. built the ark

_____ 19. ruled by a pharaoh

_____ 20. ancient country in northeastern Africa

Multiple Choice

Directions: For each numbered item, circle the letter beside the choice (A, B, C, or D) that best answers the question or completes the statement. Circle only one choice per item. Each correct answer is worth 4 points. 40 possible points.

1. Why did the descendants of Adam and Eve have reason to hope despite the terrible effects of original sin?

A. If they tried hard enough, they could obey God perfectly.
B. Their sacrifices would save them from their sins.
C. God had promised that a descendant of Eve would crush the serpent's head.
D. The Devil had decided to leave them alone.

2. Why was God displeased with Cain's sacrifice?

A. God preferred animal sacrifices to plant sacrifices.
B. Cain sacrificed too often.
C. God had always disliked Cain.
D. Cain did not give his gift with a pure heart.

3. How was Cain's attitude about his sin like that of his parents?

A. He repented right away.
B. He tried to avoid blame and to hide what he had done.
C. He took responsibility for his sin immediately.
D. He confessed his sin and asked for forgiveness.

4. When God warned Noah that he would destroy the wicked, how did He plan to do it?

A. with a great flood
B. with earthquakes
C. with a great firestorm
D. with plagues

5. What was the size of the ark?

A. The Bible doesn't tell us the size of the ark.
B. It was big enough for Noah's family only.
C. It was the size of a sailing ship.
D. It was as long as two city blocks, as wide as four houses, and as high as a five-story building.

6. Which of the following did Noah *not* bring into the ark?

A. his family
B. males and females of every kind of animal
C. his neighbors
D. food enough to feed all on the ark

7. How long did the rain fall that created the flood?

A. forty days and forty nights
B. a week
C. a year
D. a hundred days and a hundred nights

8. After the rain stopped, how did Noah keep track of how far the waters had gone down?

A. He sent out a dove.
B. He let down an anchor.
C. He used a telescope.
D. He calculated the amount of water by the number of days that had passed.

9. What sign did God give of his promise not to destroy the world again with a flood?

A. a comet
B. a shooting star
C. fire from heaven
D. a rainbow

10. A series of powerful kingdoms arose within Mesopotamia; among them were:

A. the Babylonian and Assyrian kingdoms.
B. the Egyptian and Hittite kingdoms.
C. the Canaanite and Philistine kingdoms.
D. all of the above.

PART TWO
How God Founded the Nation From Which the Redeemer of the World Came

CHAPTER 3
Abraham and Isaac

Textbook pages: 35–48
Perfect score: 100

Your Score: _____

Matching

Directions: In each blank beside a phrase, write the letter of the term that is described by that phrase. You may match more than one description to a single term. Each item is worth 3 points. 60 possible points.

A. Abraham
B. Sarah
C. Ur
D. Sodom
E. Lot

F. Melchizedek
G. Canaan
H. Hagar
I. Ishmael

J. Lot's wife
K. Isaac
L. Moriah
M. Rebecca

_____ 1. Abraham's nephew

_____ 2. the land God promised to Abraham

_____ 3. priest-king of Salem

_____ 4. a wicked city destroyed by God

_____ 5. Abraham's elderly wife

_____ 6. the land where Abraham went to offer Isaac as a sacrifice

_____ 7. was an image of Jesus Christ, who offers us the Eucharist

_____ 8. means "father of many nations"

_____ 9. a city of the Chaldeans where Abraham lived

_____ 10. Abraham and Hagar's son

_____ 11. Sarah's Egyptian servant maid

_____ 12. Isaac's wife

_____ 13. rescued Lot and all his people from captivity

_____ 14. means "princess"

_____ 15. the father of the Chosen People

_____ 16. lived the life of a nomad chief

_____ 17. Abraham and Sarah's son

_____ 18. God promised him descendants as countless as the stars

_____ 19. was turned into a pillar of salt

_____ 20. offered a sacrifice of bread and wine

Multiple Choice

Directions: For each numbered item, circle the letter beside the choice (A, B, C, or D) that best answers the question or completes the statement. Circle only one choice per item. Each correct answer is worth 4 points. 40 possible points.

1. Why did Abraham journey from his native land to Canaan?

A. There was a famine in his native land.
B. God commanded him to do it.
C. He was a refugee from war in his native land.
D. He needed better pasture land for his flocks.

2. What did God promise to Abraham?

A. He would become the father of a great nation.
B. He would give a land to him and his descendants forever.
C. Through him, all the families of the earth would be blessed.
D. All of the above.

3. When Abraham showed hospitality to the three strangers passing by his tent, what did they tell him?

A. Sarah would soon have a son.
B. Ishmael was the fulfillment of God's promise to Abraham.
C. Abraham should return to his native land.
D. Abraham would no longer be a poor man.

4. Why did Abraham try to bargain with God?

A. He wanted more land to call his own.
B. He wanted to live a long life.
C. He wanted another wife.
D. He wanted Lot and his family to escape God's wrath against their city.

5. How were Lot and his daughters saved from destruction?

A. The flaming sulfur didn't fall on their home as it did on the rest of the city.
B. They were warned to flee in a dream.
C. God decided not to destroy their city.
D. Angels took them by the hand and led them out of the city.

6. Why did Lot's wife perish?

A. She refused to leave the city because she wanted to stay with her friends.
B. She didn't believe that God would actually destroy the city.
C. She disobeyed God's instructions given by the angels.
D. She became ill and couldn't escape.

7. Why did Hagar and her son leave Abraham's people?

A. She wanted to go back to her family in Egypt.
B. Sarah was jealous of her and insisted that she leave.
C. Abraham didn't want to support Hagar and her son anymore.
D. Hagar and her son were sold to slave traders.

8. Why did God tell Abraham to offer Isaac as a sacrifice?

A. He wanted to test Abraham's faith and obedience.
B. He was punishing Abraham for disobedience.
C. He was punishing Isaac for disobedience.
D. Abraham hadn't made enough sacrifices.

9. How did Abraham's servant find the right wife for Isaac?

A. He went to the local matchmaker for advice.
B. He held a contest to see which woman was the most beautiful.
C. He asked Isaac to make the choice for himself.
D. He asked God to show him the right woman, and God answered his prayer.

10. Which of the following is a *foreshadowing* of Jesus' saving death for the world?

A. the destruction of Sodom and Gomorrah
B. Hagar's fleeing into the desert
C. Abraham's attempt to offer Isaac as a sacrifice
D. the confusion of languages at the tower of Babel

CHAPTER 4
Jacob, the Son of Isaac

Textbook pages: 49–58
Perfect score: 100

Your Score: _____

Matching

Directions: In each blank beside a phrase, write the letter of the term that is described by that phrase. You may match more than one description to a single term. Each item is worth 3 points. 60 possible points.

A. Jacob   D. Mamre   G. Peniel   J.   Rachel
B. Esau   E. Rebecca   H. Laban   K. Benjamin
C. Bethel   F. Leah   I.   Isaac

_____ 1. deceived her husband to benefit her son

_____ 2. had twelve sons

_____ 3. sold his birthright

_____ 4. Jacob's father-in-law

_____ 5. the younger twin

_____ 6. the wife Jacob worked fourteen years to gain

_____ 7. Jacob's youngest son

_____ 8. a herdsman

_____ 9. was deceived by his son and wife

_____ 10. wrestled with an angel

_____ 11. means "House of God"

_____ 12. Isaac's firstborn son

_____ 13. a hunter and farmer

question continued on next page ➡

_____ 14. Rebecca's favorite son

_____ 15. the sister of Rachel

_____ 16. saw in a dream a ladder reaching from earth to heaven

_____ 17. means "the face of God"

_____ 18. received the name "Israel"

_____ 19. a large man, rough and hairy

_____ 20. where Sarah, Abraham, Isaac, and Rebecca were buried

Multiple Choice

Directions: For each numbered item, circle the letter beside the choice (A, B, C, or D) that best answers the question or completes the statement. Circle only one choice per item. Each correct answer is worth 4 points. 40 possible points.

1. In the time of Jacob, what did the oldest son receive as part of his birthright?

A. He was given a larger portion of his father's wealth than the other children.
B. He became the head and priest of the family.
C. He obtained a special blessing from his father before he died.
D. All of the above.

2. How did Rebecca help her son deceive her husband to receive his blessing?

A. She lied to her husband.
B. She sent the older son away to a distant city.
C. She covered her younger son's neck and hands with animal skins.
D. She hid her younger son under his father's bed.

3. How could Isaac be so easily deceived?

A. He was blind.
B. He was deaf.
C. He had lost his powers of reason.
D. Both A and B above.

4. What was Esau's reaction to his mistreatment by his brother?

A. He plotted to get back the birthright and blessing for himself.
B. He hated his brother and wanted to kill him.
C. He forgave his brother right away.
D. He declared that he would never again speak to his brother.

5. How did Jacob protect himself after provoking his brother's anger?

A. He hid himself in a cave.
B. He tied up his brother while he was sleeping.
C. He bribed his brother not to hurt him.
D. He fled to his uncle's home in another city.

6. What did Jacob dream about at Bethel?

A. angels ascending and descending between heaven and earth
B. the woman he would one day marry
C. his mother weeping because he was gone
D. the wealth he would one day inherit

7. At Bethel, what did God promise Jacob?

A. God promised to give him the land where he was spending the night.
B. God promised to give him untold wealth.
C. God promised to give him many descendants.
D. Both A and C above.

8. How did the deceiver Jacob come to be deceived himself?

A. Laban tricked him into marrying both of his daughters.
B. Esau told him not to leave home because all was forgiven.
C. Isaac was only pretending when he gave Jacob his blessing.
D. Rebecca actually loved Esau more than Jacob, so she was trying to get Jacob in trouble.

9. As Jacob returned to his native land, how did he expect Esau to receive him?

A. He thought Esau would have forgotten all about how Jacob had wronged him.
B. He thought Esau would harm him and his family in revenge.
C. He thought he could gain Esau's favor with valuable gifts.
D. Both B and C above.

10. Why did Jacob receive a new name?

A. His father had named him Jacob, but his mother preferred a different name.
B. He didn't like his old name.
C. It was a sign that he had prevailed in his struggles.
D. His friends decided to give him a nickname.

CHAPTER 5
Joseph, the Son of Jacob

Textbook pages: 59–73
Perfect score: 100

Your Score: _____

Matching

Directions: In each blank beside a phrase, write the letter of the term that is described by that phrase. You may match more than one description to a single term. Each item is worth 3 points. 60 possible points.

A. Joseph
B. Esau
C. Pharaoh
D. Pharaoh's baker
E. Manasseh
F. Goshen
G. Potiphar
H. Reuben
I. Simeon
J. Pharaoh's butler
K. Benjamin
L. Canaan
M. Ephraim

_____ 1. the ruler of Egypt

_____ 2. Joseph's oldest brother, who wanted to save his life

_____ 3. appointed to a position second only to Pharaoh

_____ 4. dreamed of a vine full of grapes

_____ 5. the chief captain of Pharaoh's guard

_____ 6. Joseph's little brother

_____ 7. Jacob's youngest son

_____ 8. was accused of stealing a silver cup

_____ 9. was resented by his brothers

question continued on next page ➡

_____ 10. dreamed of three cake baskets

_____ 11. sold as a slave

_____ 12. kept in prison until his brothers returned with Benjamin

_____ 13. Jacob's homeland, where he asked to be buried

_____ 14. dreamed of the sun, moon, and stars bowing before him

_____ 15. a district in Egypt where the family of Jacob settled

_____ 16. dreamed of fat and lean cows

_____ 17. Joseph's younger son

_____ 18. interpreted dreams

_____ 19. put in prison because he was falsely accused

_____ 20. Joseph's older son

Multiple Choice

Directions: For each numbered item, circle the letter beside the choice (A, B, C, or D) that best answers the question or completes the statement. Circle only one choice per item. Each correct answer is worth 4 points. 40 possible points.

1. Why did Joseph's brothers resent him?

A. He reported their wrongdoing to their father.
B. They were jealous of him because their father showed him special favor.
C. He told them his dreams, which indicated that he would one day rule over them.
D. All of the above.

2. How did Joseph get to Egypt?

A. His father sent him there to buy food during a famine in Canaan.
B. He was sold as a slave to merchants who were on their way to Egypt.
C. He went there to find a wife.
D. He traveled there to sell goods for his family business.

3. How did Jacob's sons deceive him?

A. They showed him Joseph's coat, stained with blood.
B. They told him that Joseph had run away from home.
C. They told him that Joseph had drowned.
D. They told him that they simply couldn't find Joseph.

4. How do we know that Joseph was gifted as an administrator?

A. Potiphar placed Joseph in charge of his house.
B. The keeper of the prison placed Joseph in charge of the other prisoners.
C. Pharaoh appointed Joseph as governor.
D. All of the above.

5. Why was Joseph put in prison?

A. He was sold as a slave to the prison keeper.
B. His master believed lies about what he had done.
C. He had stolen food to stay alive because of the famine.
D. He had displeased the Pharaoh.

6. How did Joseph get out of prison?

A. He bribed the prison keeper to let him go.
B. He escaped in the middle of the night.
C. Pharaoh summoned Joseph to interpret his dreams.
D. Joseph's family arranged for his release.

7. In Pharaoh's first dream, why did the cows who represented the harvest come up out of the Nile?

A. Cows were worshipped in ancient Egypt.
B. The cows had been cooling in the river.
C. The cows had been drinking at the river's edge.
D. The harvest in Egypt depended on how high the river flooded.

8. What brought Joseph's brothers to Egypt?

A. They hoped to find Joseph and bring him home.
B. God commanded them in a dream to go to Egypt.
C. The famine had spread to Canaan, and they had heard that Egypt had food.
D. Their father had discovered their deception and disinherited them.

9. Why didn't Joseph tell his brothers who he was right away?

A. He planned to take revenge on them by having them executed.
B. He wanted to test them to find out what they would say and do.
C. He planned to bring them to justice by putting them all in prison.
D. He was secretly mocking them.

10. Why was Joseph able to forgive his brothers for mistreating him?

A. He realized that in the end God's plan made use of their wrongdoing to save his family from starvation.
B. He knew that what they had done to him wasn't really wrong.
C. He realized that the whole episode had been one big misunderstanding.
D. His father told Joseph he must forgive his brothers if he ever wanted to see his father again.

PART THREE
How God Protected His Chosen People and Led Them Into the Promised Land

CHAPTER 6
God Calls Moses to Lead His People

Textbook pages: 75–87
Perfect score: 100

Your Score: _____

Matching

Directions: In each blank beside a phrase, write the letter of the term that is described by that phrase. You may match more than one description to a single term. Each item is worth 3 points. 36 possible points.

A. Miriam
B. Moses
C. Goshen
D. Mount Horeb
E. Exodus
F. Aaron
G. Midian
H. Zipporah
I. Pharaoh

_____ 1. the wife of Moses

_____ 2. refused to let God's people go

_____ 3. the older sister of Moses

_____ 4. the place where the burning bush was found

_____ 5. the brother of Moses

_____ 6. Moses' place of refuge in the region of Mount Sinai

7. raised in Pharaoh's palace

question continued on next page ➡

_____ 8. a district in Egypt where the family of Jacob settled

_____ 9. placed in a basket on the Nile River

_____ 10. called by God to become Moses' spokesman

_____ 11. talked with God at the burning bush

_____ 12. the Hebrews' departure from slavery in Egypt

Name the Plagues

Directions: Write the names of the first 9 plagues (described in this chapter) that God brought to Egypt in the space provided below. (The tenth plague is described in the next chapter.) Each plague correctly named is worth 2 points. If you name them in the order in which they occurred, you will earn an additional 6 points. Total of 24 possible points.

1. _____

2. _____

3. _____

4. _____

5. _____

6. _____

7. _____

8. _____

9. _____

Multiple Choice

Directions: For each numbered item, circle the letter beside the choice (A, B, C, or D) that best answers the question or completes the statement. Circle only one choice per item. Each correct answer is worth 4 points. 40 possible points.

1. Which term has been used to identify descendants of Abraham, God's chosen people?

A. Israelites
B. Hebrews
C. Jews
D. all of the above

2. Jacob's clan settled in Egypt at the invitation of the Pharaoh. So how did their descendants come to be enslaved and oppressed there?

A. Later Pharaohs who came to power were jealous of the strength and wealth of the Hebrews.
B. The later Pharaohs feared that these settlers from Canaan might still have close ties to other peoples outside of Egypt who were rivals for Egyptian power and wealth.
C. The later Pharaohs needed slave laborers to build their temples, canals, and cities.
D. All of the above.

3. When Pharaoh ordered that every Hebrew boy should be killed as soon as he was born, how did Moses' mother protect him?

A. She sent him away to Canaan.
B. She hid him at home until he was an adult.
C. She pretended that he was an Egyptian orphan that she was caring for.
D. She placed him in a basket and sent it downriver on the Nile, praying that God would take care of him.

4. How did Moses come to be trained for leadership in his youth?

A. Pharaoh's daughter adopted him, so he was raised in the royal court.
B. He became a servant in the house of Pharaoh's chief general.
C. He was a natural leader who showed great skills in public speaking.
D. He was appointed to organize the labor projects of the Hebrew slaves.

5. What happened to Moses at the burning bush on the mountain?

A. He put out the fire and kept his sheep from getting hurt.
B. God gave him the mission to lead his people to freedom.
C. He offered the sacrifice of a lamb to God.
D. God spoke to him in a dream, promising him a new home for his descendants.

6. Who was appointed by God to speak for Moses?

A. Miriam
B. Zipporah
C. Aaron
D. Jethro

7. God gave Moses three miraculous signs he could use to prove to the Hebrews that he was to be their leader. Which of the following was *not* one of those signs?

A. Moses' staff turned into a serpent, and then back again into a staff.
B. Moses' hand was covered with leprosy, then was instantly healed again.
C. The Nile River dried up.
D. Some water that Moses took from the Nile River turned into blood.

8. When Moses' request angered Pharaoh, what new burden did he place on the Hebrew slaves to punish them?

A. The slaves' food rations were reduced.
B. The slaves had to make twice as many bricks.
C. In addition to making bricks, the slaves had to gather the straw needed to make the bricks.
D. The slaves' Sabbath rest day was taken away.

9. Why did God send ten plagues on the Egyptians to force Pharaoh to let the people go, instead of just one plague?

A. Pharaoh was stubborn and kept refusing to grant Moses' request.
B. God wanted to punish the Egyptian people.
C. God didn't know which kind of plague would convince Pharaoh until He had tried them all.
D. All of the above.

10. How were the Hebrews spared from the first nine plagues that God sent?

A. They weren't spared; God wanted to punish the Hebrews, too, for their disbelief.
B. The plagues did not extend to the part of Egypt where the Hebrews lived.
C. The Hebrews had magical spells they could cast to protect themselves.
D. Both B and C above.

CHAPTER 7
The Escape From Egypt

Textbook pages: 89–97
Perfect score: 100

Your Score: _____

Matching

Directions: In each blank beside a phrase, write the letter of the term that is described by that phrase. Each item is worth 4 points. 40 possible points.

A. Marah
B. Rephidim
C. Hur
D. Passover
E. Jethro
F. manna
G. Amalekites
H. Joseph
I. Red Sea
J. quail

_____ 1. campsite at the foot of Mount Horeb

_____ 2. where the Egyptians were defeated

_____ 3. provided by God to the Hebrews each evening for food

_____ 4. the night when the Hebrews were spared the tenth and final plague

_____ 5. held up one of Moses' arms during a battle

_____ 6. Moses' father-in-law

_____ 7. means "bitterness"

_____ 8. a band of warlike nomads, descendants of Esau

_____ 9. miraculous food provided to the Hebrews each morning by God

_____ 10. his body was carried back home to Canaan by his descendants

Multiple Choice

Directions: For each numbered item, circle the letter beside the choice (A, B, C, or D) that best answers the question or completes the statement. Circle only one choice per item. Each correct answer is worth 6 points. 60 possible points.

1. If the Hebrews were poor slaves, how were they able to pay for the things they needed to make their journey from Egypt after they were freed?

A. Pharaoh paid them for their many years of labor.
B. The Egyptians gave them gold, silver, and valuable clothing before they left.
C. They borrowed the money from their neighbors.
D. All of the above.

2. What was the tenth and most terrible plague that God sent upon the Egyptians?

A. the death of the firstborn children
B. an earthquake that destroyed all the cities
C. burning sulfur falling from heaven
D. leprosy

3. How were the Hebrews protected from the tenth plague?

A. by gathering inside one of the pyramids for safety
B. by singing psalms of praise to God
C. by warrior angels who guarded their homes
D. by the blood of a sacrificial lamb sprinkled on the doorframes of their homes

4. To this day, the Jews remember how God freed them from slavery and death in Egypt when they celebrate:

A. the Feast of Pentecost.
B. the Feast of Booths.
C. the Feast of Passover.
D. Yom Kippur.

5. To lead the Hebrews out of Egypt and toward the Promised Land, the Lord appeared to them by night as a pillar of fire, and by day as a pillar of:

A. smoke.
B. salt.
C. cloud.
D. light.

6. How did the Hebrews get across the Red Sea to escape the Egyptian army?

A. They built a bridge over the most narrow part of the water.
B. God parted the waters, and they went across on dry land.
C. They waded through the most shallow part of the water.
D. They sailed across in boats they had taken from the Egyptians.

7. When the people murmured against Moses in the desert and complained that they were hungry, how did God respond?

A. He let them die of starvation to punish them.
B. He sent wild beasts to devour them.
C. He provided them food through a miracle.
D. He left them alone to fend for themselves.

8. Why did God command the people to gather two days' portions of the manna on the sixth day of each week?

A. After working all week, they were usually more hungry on the sixth day.
B. That way, they wouldn't have to work to gather food on the seventh day, the day of rest.
C. They had a big feast on the sixth day of each week.
D. All of the above.

9. When the people complained in the desert that they were thirsty and had no water, how did God quench their thirst?

A. When Moses struck a rock at God's command, water came gushing out of it.
B. God caused it to rain in the desert.
C. God showed Moses where to find an oasis with water.
D. Both B and C above.

10. How did the Hebrews win their battle with the Amalekites?

A. The Hebrews ambushed the Amalekites between two mountains.
B. The Amalekites saw warrior angels fighting for the Hebrews, so they fled in terror.
C. The Hebrews outnumbered the Amalekites ten to one.
D. As long as Moses held his staff over his head and prayed for victory, the Israelites were successful.

CHAPTER 8
The Revelation of God's Law

Textbook pages: 99–112
Perfect score: 100

Your Score: _____

Matching

Directions: In each blank beside a phrase, write the letter of the term that is best described by that phrase. Each item is worth 2 points. 50 possible points.

A. Mount Sinai
B. seven-branched candlestick
C. unbloody sacrifices
D. Tabernacle
E. holocausts
F. breastplate
G. peace offerings
H. Joshua
I. ephod

J. sin offerings
K. miter
L. Feast of Trumpets
M. bloody sacrifices
N. mercy seat
O. oblation
P. sabbatical year
Q. Ark of the Covenant
R. trespass offerings

S. table of showbreads
T. Holy of Holies
U. Day of Atonement
V. Feast of the Pasch
W. Feast of Booths
X. azymes
Y. Feast of Pentecost

_____ 1. various kinds of plant foods offered as sacrifices to God

_____ 2. a room containing the Ark of the Covenant

_____ 3. a square of cloth worn by the priest, with twelve precious stones bearing the names of the twelve tribes

_____ 4. every seventh year, when sowing and reaping the fields were forbidden

_____ 5. a day of thanksgiving to God for the harvest and the increase of the flocks

_____ 6. the great day of public penance and fasting, when no work was done

_____ 7. made of acacia wood and covered with gold, holding six loaves

_____ 8. celebrated in thanksgiving for the fruit harvest, and in memory of the Hebrews' dwelling in tents in the wilderness

_____ 9. the golden cover for the Ark of the covenant, with two golden images of angels

question continued on next page ➡

_____ 10. the place where God gave the Law to Moses

_____ 11. a crown-shaped cap worn by the priest

_____ 12. any offering to God

_____ 13. animals slain as sacrificial offerings to God

_____ 14. sacrifices to make satisfaction for serious sins; also known as expiatory offerings

_____ 15. a great tent where the people gathered to worship

_____ 16. sacrificial animal victims offered entirely to God by being consumed with fire

_____ 17. the priest's outermost garment

_____ 18. celebrated on the new moon of the seventh month of each year with a number of animal sacrifices

_____ 19. sacrifices made for lesser, or venial, sins

_____ 20. sacrifices made as acts of thanksgiving or petition to God

_____ 21. another name for Passover

_____ 22. unleavened bread

_____ 23. the light for the sanctuary of the Tabernacle

_____ 24. held up one of Moses' arms during a battle

_____ 25. a large box made of acacia wood and lined inside and outside with gold

Multiple Choice

Directions: For each numbered item, circle the letter beside the choice (A, B, C, or D) that best answers the question or completes the statement. Circle only one choice per item. Each correct answer is worth 5 points. 50 possible points.

1. How did God prepare the Israelites to receive the Law through Moses?
A. He asked them whether or not they would be obedient to the Law.
B. He promised them that if they were obedient, He would make them His chosen people.

question continued on next page ➡

C. He instructed them to consecrate themselves for two days by washing themselves and their clothes so they could focus on Him in worship and prayer.

D. All of the above.

2. What did the people see and hear at Mount Sinai when God gave the Law?

A. lightning, thunder, and a heavy cloud

B. a trumpet blast, an earthquake, and thick smoke

C. brilliant sunlight and a rainbow

D. both A and B above

3. Which of the following is *not* one of the Ten Commandments that God gave the Israelites?

A. "You shall take the name of the Lord your God in vain."

B. "You shall not kill."

C. "Remember the Sabbath day, to keep it holy."

D. "Honor your father and your mother."

4. Which of the following is *not* one of the Ten Commandments that God gave the Israelites?

A. "You shall not covet your neighbor's house."

B. "You shall not forgive a mortal sin."

C. "You shall not steal."

D. "You shall not bear false witness against your neighbor."

5. In what written form did God give the Law to Moses?

A. on a parchment scroll, written in the blood of a lamb

B. carved into the wood of the Ark of the Covenant

C. inscribed on two stone tablets

D. inscribed on two clay tablets

6. When Moses stayed up on the mountain with God for forty days and nights, how did the people respond?

A. They hoped and prayed that Moses would be safe.

B. They sent a rescue party up the mountain to search for Moses.

C. They thought God had abandoned them, so they worshipped an idol instead.

D. They thought that Moses had died, so they chose a new leader.

7. Which of the following is *not* a reason why God gave the Israelites the Law?

A. to teach them how to be holy

B. to show them how to worship Him

C. to remind them to be sorry for their sins

D. to help them be accepted by the surrounding peoples

8. Again, which of the following is *not* a reason why God gave the Israelites the Law?

A. to keep them from becoming like the nations that worshipped false gods
B. to show which of them didn't really belong to the Chosen People
C. to remind them to be thankful
D. to point toward the Savior who was to come centuries later

9. The animal on whom the high priest laid his hands while confessing the sins of the people was called:

A. the scapegoat.
B. the Paschal lamb.
C. the holocaust.
D. the golden calf.

10. In many ways the ancient worship rituals of the Israelites serve as the roots of our Christian worship because:

A. several centuries after Jesus's death and resurrection, the Church discovered and imitated Jewish rituals.
B. the early Christians didn't have any worship rituals, so they imitated what they saw the Jewish people doing.
C. Jesus Christ was the fulfillment of God's promise to His chosen people.
D. all of the above.

CHAPTER 9
The Desert Wanderings of the Israelites

Textbook pages: 113–123
Perfect score: 100

Your Score: _____

Matching

Directions: In each blank beside a phrase, write the letter of the term that is described by that phrase. Each item is worth 4 points. 40 possible points.

A. Balaam
B. the Wilderness of Sin
C. Korah, Dathan, and Abiram
D. Eleazar
E. Joshua and Caleb
F. Hebron
G. Miriam
H. Balak
I. Joshua
J. Mount Nebo

_____ 1. where Moses died

_____ 2. the only Israelite scouts who lived to take part in the conquest of Canaan

_____ 3. king of the Moabites

_____ 4. the lieutenant of Moses who led the people after Moses died

_____ 5. stricken with leprosy for rebelling against Moses

_____ 6. Aaron's son, who became the high priest after him

_____ 7. where the Israelite scouts found a giant cluster of grapes

_____ 8. a prophet from Mesopotamia

_____ 9. rebels who were swallowed up by the earth for their rebellion

_____ 10. the Israelites had to pass through here to enter the Promised Land

Multiple Choice

Directions: For each numbered item, circle the letter beside the choice (A, B, C, or D) that best answers the question or completes the statement. Circle only one choice per item. Each correct answer is worth 6 points. 60 possible points.

1. When the Israelites broke camp to continue their journey through the wilderness, how did they travel?

A. The younger adults could march faster than the older ones, so they led the march.
B. The people marched in an orderly procession, with each tribe in their assigned order, and with the Ark of the Covenant carried first and the materials of the Tabernacle next.
C. One tribe went ahead of the others to scout out the land, and the others followed when they received word that it was safe.
D. The men of all the tribes marched first, followed by the women and children.

2. What chastisements did God send to the people because of their rebellion, complaining, and ingratitude?

A. fire
B. plague
C. venomous snakes
D. all of the above

3. Before they entered Canaan, God commanded Moses to choose twelve men, one from each tribe, so they could:

A. form a council to help him govern the people.
B. establish a new priesthood.
C. scout out the enemy territory as spies.
D. settle a new town on the border of the land.

4. Why did the Israelites refuse to enter the Promised Land once they had finally arrived there?

A. They feared the people who already lived there.
B. They thought the land was barren and couldn't be farmed.
C. They found the nearby land of Moab more desirable.
D. They had grown accustomed to living in the desert.

5. When the Israelites disobeyed God and refused to enter Canaan, what was their punishment?

A. They were all defeated in battle and enslaved by the Amalekites.
B. Their children were denied entrance to the Promised Land.
C. The older generation was condemned to linger in the desert until they died.
D. They all died of starvation because the manna stopped appearing.

6. What was the sign that Aaron's priesthood placed him above all the other leaders except Moses?

A. A light from the heavens shone on Aaron and made his face radiant.
B. God caused Aaron's wooden staff to bloom miraculously.
C. Aaron's hair suddenly turned bright white.
D. Aaron received a beautiful robe of many colors.

7. Why was Moses not allowed by God to enter the Promised Land?

A. Moses had disobeyed God by the way he gave the people water at Kadesh.
B. Moses had grown too old for the final part of the journey.
C. God had a new mission for Moses to complete back in Egypt.
D. Moses had questioned why God wanted him to enter the Promised Land.

8. How were the Israelites saved from venomous snakes in the Wilderness of Sin?

A. When those who were bitten drank the waters gushing from the rock, they were healed.
B. They set fire to the snakes' dens and killed them all.
C. A miraculous flood appeared suddenly and washed the snakes away.
D. When those who were bitten looked at the bronze snake that Moses had made at God's command, they were healed.

9. Why does no one today know the exact spot where Moses was buried?

A. God hid Moses' grave from the Israelites so that they wouldn't take his body and worship it.
B. God Himself buried Moses, not the people.
C. Both A and B above.
D. None of the above.

10. How did Balaam's donkey save his life?

A. When he fell deathly ill while riding her, she galloped quickly to a nearby doctor's house.
B. When he tried to eat a plant that he didn't know was poison, she kicked it out of his hand.
C. When he was being sucked down in quicksand, she pulled him out with a rope.
D. When she saw a threatening angel ahead, blocking the path, she refused to go forward.

CHAPTER 10
Joshua, Commander of the Israelites

Textbook pages: 125–135
Perfect score: 100

Your Score: _____

Matching

Directions: In each blank beside a phrase, write the letter of the term that is described by that phrase. Each item is worth 4 points. 40 possible points.

A. Phoenicians
B. Philistines
C. Achan
D. Edomites
E. Syrians
F. Phinehas
G. Rahab
H. Jordan
I. Moabites
J. Amorites

_____ 1. a nomadic people who had wandered from Arabia and made settlements throughout Mesopotamia

_____ 2. hid the Israelite spies in Jericho

_____ 3. disobeyed God by retaining some of the treasures of Jericho for himself

_____ 4. lived in the country bordering on the east coast of the Dead Sea

_____ 5. the son of Eleazar, whom he succeeded as high priest

_____ 6. a nation that God allowed the Israelites to destroy, so that His people would not imitate their life of idolatry

_____ 7. the first people to develop an alphabet

_____ 8. lived south of the Dead Sea and were hostile to the Israelites

_____ 9. the most important river in Canaan

_____ 10. the most powerful of the tribes who lived in Canaan when the Israelites arrived

Multiple Choice

Directions: For each numbered item, circle the letter beside the choice (A, B, C, or D) that best answers the question or completes the statement. Circle only one choice per item. Each correct answer is worth 6 points. 60 possible points.

1. The land of Canaan is about as large as the modern American state of:

A. Rhode Island.
B. Maryland.
C. Texas.
D. Alaska.

2. To the east of Canaan lay:

A. the mountainous lands of what is now Lebanon.
B. the coastal area of the Mediterranean Sea.
C. the Dead Sea and the great Eastern Desert.
D. the Sinai Desert, a part of Egypt.

3. To the south of Canaan lay:

A. the mountainous lands of what is now Lebanon.
B. the coastal area of the Mediterranean Sea.
C. the Dead Sea and the great Eastern Desert.
D. the Sinai Desert, a part of Egypt.

4. To the west of Canaan lay:

A. the mountainous lands of what is now Lebanon.
B. the coastal area of the Mediterranean Sea.
C. the Dead Sea and the great Eastern Desert.
D. the Sinai Desert, a part of Egypt.

5. To the north of Canaan lay:

A. the mountainous lands of what is now Lebanon.
B. the coastal area of the Mediterranean Sea.
C. the Dead Sea and the great Eastern Desert.
D. the Sinai Desert, a part of Egypt.

6. There were two seasons in Canaan:

A. summer and winter.
B. spring and fall.
C. the cold season and the wet season.
D. the rainy season and the dry season.

7. Which of the peoples already settled in Palestine when the Israelites arrived used superior weapons made of iron instead of bronze?

A. the Edomites
B. the Moabites
C. the Philistines
D. the Amorites

8. How did the Israelites cross the Jordan River into Canaan?

A. Joshua lifted his staff over the waters as Moses had done at the Red Sea, and the waters parted so the people could cross.
B. They built small boats from the wood of nearby trees.
C. The priests carried the Ark of the Covenant into the river, and a dry path appeared for the people to cross.
D. They built a rope bridge to cross over.

9. Which enemy city's walls fell down after the Israelites marched around it, blew trumpets, and shouted?

A. Ai
B. Shechem
C. Hebron
D. Jericho

10. How did Joshua secure a victory over the Amorites at Gibeon?

A. At his command, the sun and moon both stood still, giving him the extra time he needed.
B. The Edomites, who hated the Amorites, suddenly appeared on the battlefield to help him win.
C. Warrior angels drove the Amorites into an ambush.
D. The Israelites used iron weapons that were superior to the bronze weapons of the Amorites.

CHAPTER 11
The Israelites in the Promised Land

Textbook pages: 137–152
Perfect score: 100

Your Score: _____

Matching

Directions: In each blank beside a phrase, write the letter of the term that is described by that phrase. Each item is worth 4 points. 40 possible points.

A. Gideon
B. Hannah
C. Deborah
D. Gaza
E. Baal
F. judge
G. Delilah
H. Ruth
I. Samuel
J. Samson

_____ 1. the mother of Samuel

_____ 2. an angel foretold his birth to his mother

_____ 3. Samson loved her, but she betrayed him

_____ 4. showed great kindness and faithfulness to her mother-in-law

_____ 5. a type of military leader who ruled only during a time of trouble

_____ 6. God called his name while he was sleeping in the Tabernacle

_____ 7. a Philistine city

_____ 8. the only woman noted in the Bible to have served the Israelite people as a judge

_____ 9. a false god worshipped by some of the pagan peoples of Canaan

_____ 10. asked for a sign from the Lord to guarantee what He promised

Multiple Choice

Directions: For each numbered item, circle the letter beside the choice (A, B, C, or D) that best answers the question or completes the statement. Circle only one choice per item. Each correct answer is worth 6 points. 60 possible points.

1. Which of the following peoples were *not* one of the principal adversaries of the Israelites in Canaan?

A. the Hittites
B. the Ammonites
C. the Egyptians
D. the Midianites

2. Why did God permit the enemies of the Israelites to make war against them from time to time?

A. He was chastising the Israelites for failing to keep His commandments after they settled into their new life in Canaan.
B. He had changed His mind and no longer wanted the Israelites to live in Canaan.
C. Once their enemies conquered the Israelites, they could live together in peace as one people.
D. None of the above.

3. What did God tell Gideon to do with the army of thirty-two thousand men he had raised to protect the Israelites?

A. God told Gideon to arm them with swords and shields for the battle.
B. God told Gideon to choose from among them only three hundred men for the task.
C. God told Gideon to divide them into two armies so they could attack the enemy on two sides.
D. God told Gideon to march them into battle with the Ark of the Covenant carried before them.

4. What unlikely weapons were used by the Israelites to defeat the Midianites in the Valley of Esdraelon?

A. slings and nets
B. burning oil and pitch
C. trumpets, pitchers, and lamps
D. warrior elephants

5. Why did Gideon refuse to be made king of the Israelites?

A. He thought he was too old to become king.
B. He had no leadership skills.
C. He didn't want the heavy responsibilities of being a king.
D. They had the Lord to be their king rather than a man.

6. How did the judge named Samson attack the Philistines?

A. He led a well-equipped army of twenty thousand men.
B. He depended on his own tremendous physical strength.
C. He made an alliance with the Ammonites.
D. He infiltrated their camp by night with a small team of special forces.

7. What unusual weapons did Samson use against the Philistines?

A. flaming foxes
B. the jawbone of a donkey
C. the roof and pillars of a banquet hall
D. all of the above

8. What was the source of Samson's great strength?

A. His strength came from his hair, which had never been cut because of a vow of consecration to God.
B. An angel stood beside him at all times to fight for him.
C. He used a secret herbal formula that multiplied his strength.
D. He inherited the strength from his father and grandfather.

9. What was unusual about Samuel's birth?

A. Samuel and two brothers were born as identical triplets, but the other two died.
B. His mother had no pain when she gave birth to Samuel.
C. His mother prophesied that Samuel would be a judge and a prophet.
D. Though his mother had been unable to have children for years, Samuel was God's answer to her prayer at the Tabernacle for a son.

10. Ruth was a Moabite widow with no wealth, power, status, or fame. How did she come to have such an important role in the story of the Bible?

A. She foretold the birth of Jesus Christ in a prophecy.
B. She convinced her fellow Moabites to become Israelites who worshipped the one true God.
C. Through her great-grandson, a royal line of descendants led directly to the Savior of the world.
D. She became the only woman judge of Israel recorded in the Bible.

PART FOUR
How God's Chosen People Lived Under Their Kings

CHAPTER 12
Saul and David

Textbook pages: 153–169
Perfect score: 100

Your Score: _____

Matching

Directions: In each blank beside a phrase, write the letter of the term that is described by that phrase. You may match more than one description to a single term. Each item is worth 4 points. 40 possible points.

A. Michal
B. Jesse
C. Saul
D. Bethlehem
E. Goliath
F. Samuel
G. Jonathan
H. David
I. Endor

_____ 1. the judge who anointed the first and second kings of Israel

_____ 2. Saul's son

_____ 3. the Philistine warrior champion

_____ 4. David's father

_____ 5. the second king of Israel

_____ 6. David's wife

_____ 7. David's hometown

_____ 8. where Saul hired a witch to call up Samuel's ghost

_____ 9. the first king of Israel

_____ 10. David's best friend

Multiple Choice

Directions: For each numbered item, circle the letter beside the choice (A, B, C, or D) that best answers the question or completes the statement. Circle only one choice per item. Each correct answer is worth 6 points. 60 possible points.

1. Why did the Israelites want to be ruled by a king?

A. They wanted to be united under one leader like the other nations around them.
B. They wanted a human king to lead them to a final victory over the Canaanites and the Philistines.
C. They thought a human king would prevent civil war and ensure justice.
D. All of the above.

2. Because Saul disobeyed God, the kingship eventually passed from his family to another. How did he disobey God?

A. Saul impatiently offered a sacrifice to God before battle instead of waiting for Samuel, who was the only one authorized by God to do it.
B. Saul took for himself the plunder from a victory over the Amalekites, then spared their king, against God's command.
C. Saul married many pagan wives and worshipped their gods.
D. Both A and B above.

3. Who told Saul, "To obey is better than to sacrifice"?

A. Samuel
B. David
C. Jonathan
D. Michal

4. How did young David help Saul when Saul became sad and distressed?

A. David played a guessing game with Saul to take his mind off his troubles.
B. David told Saul exciting stories about how God had rescued the Israelites from Egypt.
C. David played the harp to entertain Saul and cheer him up.
D. David brought with him a little dog that performed tricks for Saul.

5. How did young David defeat the giant Goliath in battle?

A. David came up on Goliath secretly from behind and struck him with a sword.
B. David used Saul's armor and weapons to protect himself and then pierced Goliath with a spear.
C. David's words struck terror into Goliath's heart, and Goliath retreated.
D. David used a sling to strike Goliath in the head with a stone.

6. Why was Saul jealous of David?

A. David was more handsome than Saul.
B. Saul's wife talked often about David.
C. David's deeds in battle received more praise from the people than Saul's deeds.
D. Saul thought that God loved David more than He loved Saul.

7. How did David show that he had no desire to hurt Saul, even though Saul was hunting him down to kill him?

A. David surrendered to Saul to show his good will.
B. David could have killed Saul while he slept, but spared him instead.
C. David sent lavish gifts to Saul to show his friendship.
D. David sent messengers to Saul to declare his loyalty to him.

8. Why did Saul seek out a witch to summon the ghost of Samuel after Samuel had died?

A. Saul wanted to ask Samuel's forgiveness for his disobedience.
B. Saul wanted to curse Samuel for prophesying that someone would take Saul's place as king.
C. Saul wanted to know what he should do as he faced a great battle the next day with the Philistines.
D. Saul missed Samuel and wanted to hear his voice one last time.

9. What did the ghost of Samuel prophesy would happen to Saul?

A. Samuel predicted that the Philistines would defeat Israel, and Saul and his sons would die in battle.
B. Samuel predicted that Saul would be allowed one more victory before he died in battle.
C. Samuel predicted that Saul would live to an old age, but he would never be happy.
D. Samuel predicted that Saul and David would be reconciled and then live together in peace.

10. When David heard of Saul's death in battle:

A. he rejoiced that the man who had sought to kill him was now dead.
B. he blamed himself for not protecting Saul from the Philistines.
C. he mourned and wept and fasted until evening.
D. he immediately gathered the troops to have himself declared king of the entire nation of Israel.

CHAPTER 13
David's Reign

Textbook pages: 171–182
Perfect score: 100

Your Score: _____

Matching

Directions: In each blank beside a phrase, write the letter of the term that is described by that phrase. You may match more than one description to a single term. Each item is worth 4 points. 40 possible points.

A. Tyre
B. Jerusalem
C. Joab
D. Bathsheba
E. Absalom
F. Mount Zion
G. Hiram
H. David
I. Nathan

_____ 1. the general of David's army

_____ 2. the hill on which Jerusalem was originally built

_____ 3. David had her husband killed so he could take her as his wife

_____ 4. a prophet who rebuked David for his sins

_____ 5. the leading city of the Phoenicians

_____ 6. danced before the Ark of the Covenant, playing a harp

_____ 7. known as the City of David

_____ 8. David's son who revolted against him

_____ 9. David's capital city

_____ 10. king of the Phoenicians

Multiple Choice

Directions: For each numbered item, circle the letter beside the choice (A, B, C, or D) that best answers the question or completes the statement. Circle only one choice per item. Each correct answer is worth 6 points. 60 possible points.

1. Once David was recognized as king of the tribe of Judah, why did seven and a half years pass before the rest of the nation would accept him as their king?

A. David had no ambition to become king of the entire nation.
B. A long civil war was caused by Abner who wanted to make Saul's surviving son king.
C. God had commanded David to be patient in waiting for recognition from the other tribes.
D. David was too busy fighting the Philistines to be concerned with becoming king of the entire nation.

2. How did David establish a new capital city for his kingdom?

A. He captured a city of the Canaanites and made it his capital.
B. He built a new city using his soldiers as laborers.
C. He chose a small Israelite settlement to expand into a great city.
D. He built great walls and a fortress around a hill where his army had camped.

3. Which foreign ruler sent David cedar wood, with carpenters and masons, to build a palace for him?

A. the king of the Amorites
B. the king of the Phoenicians
C. the Egyptian pharaoh
D. the king of the Hittites

4. Why did David decide to bring the Ark of the Covenant to Mount Zion?

A. He wanted to attach the people more closely to himself and to his capital city.
B. He feared that it might be captured by the Philistines again if it stayed where it was.
C. He had built a great temple there to house the Ark.
D. He wanted to see what was hidden inside the Ark.

5. How did David's son, who revolted against him, meet his death?

A. David's forces ambushed him in a narrow valley, and when he tried to flee, the archers shot and killed him.
B. God struck him down with a fatal illness after he captured David's capital city.
C. While riding on a mule, his long hair caught in the branch of a tree and left him helplessly hanging in the air; he was killed there by David's captain.
D. He tried to escape and hide in a cave, but he was crushed to death by the falling rocks of an earthquake.

6. When David learned that his rebel son had died, how did he respond?

A. He celebrated with his army because they had won the battle.
B. He rejoiced that the young man who had tried to kill him and take his kingdom was now dead.
C. He mourned bitterly and cried out for his son.
D. He sent his soldiers to put to death anyone who had supported his son's revolt.

7. How did David's faithful soldier, Uriah, die in battle?

A. David arranged for Uriah to be left defenseless by his fellow soldiers, so that he would die and David could take Uriah's wife.
B. Uriah died bravely defending David when David was under attack by enemy warriors.
C. Uriah acted foolishly by leading an assault that failed because his men were outnumbered.
D. None of the above.

8. How did the prophet convince David that he had committed a grave sin?

A. He brought in witnesses to testify to what David had done.
B. He accused David of breaking the fifth and sixth commandments.
C. He told David he would call down God's wrath on David if he didn't repent.
D. He told him a story that showed David the evil nature of his actions.

9. Which of the following was *not* one of David's accomplishments?

A. He united the Israelites into one great nation, building up a powerful state in the process.
B. He built a magnificent Temple for the worship of God.
C. He created a large standing army with experienced commanders.
D. He organized the Levites to care for the Ark, guarded the treasures collected for the Temple, and formed a choir to chant sacred music.

10. One of David's most beautiful psalms, which he composed when Saul was persecuting him, begins with these words:

A. "I was glad when they said to me, 'Let us go to the house of the Lord!'"
B. "O Lord, our Lord, how majestic is Your name in all the earth!"
C. "The heavens are telling the glory of God."
D. "The Lord is my shepherd, I shall not want."

CHAPTER 14
The Israelites Under King Solomon

Textbook pages: 183–191
Perfect score: 100

Your Score: _____

Matching

Directions: In each blank beside a phrase, write the letter of the term that is described by that phrase. You may match more than one description to a single term. Each item is worth 2 points. 40 possible points.

A. Solomon
B. King Hiram
C. the Porch
D. the Queen of Sheba
E. Court of the Gentiles
F. the Sanctuary
G. Jeroboam
H. Court of the Priests
I. Holy of Holies
J. Court of the Israelites
K. Ahijah
L. House of the Forest of Lebanon
M. bronze basin
N. Ashtoreth
O. Hall of the Throne

_____ 1. came to Jerusalem from a foreign land to meet Solomon

_____ 2. the outermost court of the Temple

_____ 3. the wisest of all the rulers of his time

_____ 4. bowl holding about ten thousand gallons of water where the priests washed

_____ 5. the middle court of the Temple

_____ 6. in charge of the fortifications of Jerusalem

_____ 7. the son of David and Bathsheba

_____ 8. sought to lead a rebellion against Solomon

_____ 9. furnished fir and cedar trees to build the Temple

_____ 10. had the Temple built

_____ 11. has wise sayings recorded in the Book of Proverbs

_____ 12. the pagan goddess of the Sidonians

_____ 13. the next king of Israel after David

_____ 14. prophesied that Solomon's kingdom would be torn in two

_____ 15. the vestibule of the Temple

_____ 16. contained the Ark of the Covenant

_____ 17. the innermost court of the Temple

_____ 18. room in Solomon's palace where he pronounced judgments for the people

_____ 19. room containing the altar of incense, table of showbread, and seven-branched candlesticks

_____ 20. assembly hall in Solomon's palace

Multiple Choice

Directions: For each numbered item, circle the letter beside the choice (A, B, C, or D) that best answers the question or completes the statement. Circle only one choice per item. Each correct answer is worth 6 points. 60 possible points.

1. When God spoke to Solomon and asked him to name the gifts he desired, what one thing did Solomon want?

A. wealth
B. wisdom
C. power
D. fame

2. When two women in court claimed the same child as their own, how did Solomon decide which woman was the child's true mother?

A. He gathered witnesses to tell him the truth.
B. He saw that the child resembled one of the mothers more than the other.
C. He threatened to jail them both unless they told the truth.
D. The true mother was willing to give up her child rather than see the child die.

3. During the construction of the Temple, why was there no noise of a hammer?

A. Every beam and stone was carefully cut and fitted beforehand.
B. The hammers were wrapped with silk to muffle the noise.
C. The workers stuffed rags in their ears to protect their hearing.
D. All of the above.

4. What took place at the dedication of the Temple?

A. Twenty-two thousand oxen and one hundred and twenty thousand sheep were sacrificed.
B. After Solomon's prayer, fire came down from heaven to consume the sacrifices.
C. People from every part of the kingdom came to the celebration and feasted for fourteen days.
D. All of the above.

5. How did Solomon protect his kingdom and his traders?

A. He erected fortresses along the northern frontier and in the plains.
B. He paid tribute to surrounding nations who were more powerful than Israel.
C. He fortified the Temple and palace and built a city to protect his caravans coming in from the East.
D. Both A and C above.

6. In what ways did Solomon carry on trade with neighboring countries?

A. He had the Egyptian Pharaoh build commercial ships for his merchants.
B. He sent commercial ships to distant lands and built caravan routes to neighboring countries.
C. He placed armed guards around every caravan.
D. He created an international market place in Jerusalem.

7. What were the two major factors that led to the breakup of Jewish unity?

A. tribal rivalry and constant civil strife
B. famine and food shortages
C. taxation and idolatry
D. attacks by hostile neighboring nations

8. What was the one important means for keeping the people united with him that Solomon neglected?

A. building the Temple as a religious center for the nation
B. replacing the traditional tribal divisions with provinces administered from Jerusalem
C. maintaining peace with Israel's enemies through military strength
D. offering a faithful example of worshipping the one true God

9. How did the prophet who spoke to Jeroboam act out his prophesy that the nation would be divided?

A. He scooped up a handful of sand and scattered it to the wind.
B. He gathered twelve bundles of grain and burned two of them.
C. He measured out twelve vessels of water, then poured two of them on the ground.
D. He tore his robe into twelve pieces and gave ten of them to Jeroboam.

10. What pattern can we see throughout the history of the Old Testament—a pattern that still takes place today?

A. Times of happiness and prosperity are followed by periods of decline because of sin.
B. God sends His people leaders who never fail to obey Him.
C. People turn to God most often when they are happy and prosperous.
D. Both A and B above.

CHAPTER 15
Jeroboam and Rehoboam

Textbook pages: 193–198
Perfect score: 100

Your Score: _____

Matching

Directions: In each blank beside a phrase, write the letter of the term that is described by that phrase. You may match more than one description to a single term. Each item is worth 4 points. 40 possible points.

A. Kingdom of Judah
B. Jeroboam
C. Shechem
D. the Pharaoh of Egypt
E. Rehoboam
F. Abijam
G. Kingdom of Israel
H. Adoram

_____ 1. Solomon's son and successor as king

_____ 2. the Southern Kingdom

_____ 3. an overseer of the forced laborers

_____ 4. capital city of the Northern Kingdom

_____ 5. built two temples not in Jerusalem

_____ 6. Rehoboam's son and successor as king

_____ 7. the Northern Kingdom

_____ 8. founded a new state religion for the Northern Kingdom

_____ 9. stole the treasures of the Temple and the king's palace in Jerusalem

_____ 10. urged his people to worship the golden calf

Multiple Choice

Directions: For each numbered item, circle the letter beside the choice (A, B, C, or D) that best answers the question or completes the statement. Circle only one choice per item. Each correct answer is worth 6 points. 60 possible points.

1. Which two tribes remained loyal to Rehoboam?

A. Reuben and Simeon
B. Judah and Benjamin
C. Asher and Zebulon
D. Gad and Naphtali

2. How did Rehoboam provoke a rebellion against his rule?

A. He threatened to raise taxes.
B. He dismissed all the priests from their ministry.
C. He made an alliance with the Egyptians.
D. He turned the Temple into his royal palace.

3. Why did the Levites align themselves with Rehoboam?

A. Rehoboam exempted them from taxes.
B. Rehoboam promised to expand and beautify the Temple.
C. Rehoboam promised to give them new ancestral lands.
D. Jeroboam was leading his people into idolatry.

4. Why wouldn't Jeroboam allow the people of his ten tribes to worship in the Temple at Jerusalem?

A. He wanted to keep their Temple donations for himself.
B. After the kingdoms had divided, the journey to the Temple had become dangerous.
C. He wanted to keep the people loyal to himself rather than to God.
D. He feared that Rehoboam would enslave his people if they went to Jerusalem.

5. Why did Jeroboam make Shechem his capital?

A. Shechem was a well-fortified city.
B. Shechem was the largest city in his kingdom.
C. Shechem was closely connected with the founders of the Israelite nation.
D. Shechem was a wealthy city with many influential people.

6. Why did God permit the Pharaoh of Egypt to invade the Kingdom of Judah?

A. God's plan was to unite the kingdoms of Judah and Egypt.
B. Rehoboam had set an example of idolatry, and the people had followed it.
C. Pharaoh became a prisoner of war, and while in prison he came to worship the one true God.
D. As punishment for their sins, the people were to be taken back to Egypt as slaves.

7. Why did Jeroboam command his men to seize a prophet from the Kingdom of Judah?

A. He thought the prophet was a spy sent by Judah's king.
B. He thought the prophet was a fraud trying to cheat people out of their money.
C. The prophet had declared that God would punish the idolatry of Jeroboam and his people.
D. Both A and B above.

8. Why did prosperity come to an end after the kingdom was divided?

A. Neither king was strong enough to trade with other countries.
B. Civil wars ruined great portions of the country.
C. Great numbers of men taken from the trades and agriculture died as soldiers.
D. All of the above.

9. What happened to Jeroboam when he spoke against the prophet?

A. Jeroboam died suddenly.
B. Jeroboam's hand became withered.
C. Jeroboam's skin turned white with leprosy.
D. Jeroboam was struck blind.

10. When the queen of Israel went in disguise to the prophet at Shiloh, what did he tell her?

A. Her son would live to become the greatest king the Israelites had ever known.
B. Her son would die, her husband would lose his throne, and her people would be taken into captivity by the Assyrians.
C. The king of Judah would soon die, and his kingdom would fall to the Egyptians.
D. Her husband would conquer Judah and reunite the two kingdoms.

CHAPTER 16
Elijah the Prophet

Textbook pages: 199–211
Perfect score: 100

Your Score: _____

Matching

Directions: In each blank beside a phrase, write the letter of the term that is described by that phrase. Each item is worth 4 points. 40 possible points.

A. Mount Carmel
B. Jehoshaphat
C. Elisha
D. Ahab
E. Horeb
F. Samaria
G. Jezebel
H. Jordan River
I. Naaman
J. Elijah

_____ 1. the mountain of God, where Elijah lived in a cave

_____ 2. Ahab's wicked wife

_____ 3. the new capital of the Northern Kingdom

_____ 4. a prophet sent by God to Ahab

_____ 5. the place where Elijah was taken to heaven

_____ 6. the general of the Syrian army

_____ 7. a wicked king of Israel

_____ 8. the place where Elijah challenged false prophets to a contest

_____ 9. a king of Judah

_____ 10. Elijah's disciple

Multiple Choice

Directions: For each numbered item, circle the letter beside the choice (A, B, C, or D) that best answers the question or completes the statement. Circle only one choice per item. Each correct answer is worth 6 points. 60 possible points.

1. To please his wicked wife, Ahab built in Samaria:

A. a luxurious palace.
B. a temple to the pagan god Baal.
C. a stadium for blood games.
D. all of the above.

2. Why did the land of Israel suffer a great drought from three years without rain?

A. Ahab's sins of idolatry brought about this punishment on all the people.
B. Pagan priests had cursed the land.
C. God was waiting for the people to pray for rain.
D. God was testing Elijah.

3. How was Elijah fed at the brook called Cherith?

A. Nearby farmers brought him grain from their fields.
B. He caught fish in the brook.
C. God sent him manna and quail, just as He had sent them to Moses.
D. Each morning and evening a raven brought him food.

4. How did Elijah survive the three-year drought and famine?

A. He found a great storehouse of food and water hidden in a cave.
B. A widow fed him from a small supply of food that God multiplied.
C. The king supplied him food and water from the royal supplies.
D. All of the above.

5. What did Elijah do when a boy died in the household where he was staying?

A. He performed a funeral for the child and buried him.
B. He accused the neighbors of poisoning the boy.
C. He prayed for the boy, and God raised the child from the dead.
D. He prophesied that God would give the boy's mother another son.

6. How did Elijah show that his God was the true God, and Baal was not?

A. God sent fire from heaven to consume the sacrifice on His altar, but Baal could not do the same for the sacrifice on his altar.
B. Elijah cursed the prophets of Baal, and they were struck blind.
C. The prophets of Baal were struck by lightning.
D. The idol of Baal worshipped by the pagans dissolved into ashes.

7. How did Jezebel help her husband get Naboth's vineyard?

A. She offered Naboth a large sum for the vineyard, so he sold it to her.
B. She threatened to blackmail Naboth if he didn't sell it to her.
C. She appealed to Naboth's sense of patriotism, saying that the king needed it for the good of the country.
D. She arranged for Naboth to be falsely accused of a crime, and when he was stoned to death, the king took the vineyard.

8. How did Elijah's life on earth come to an end?

A. Jezebel finally captured him and put him to death.
B. He died of old age in a cave at Mount Carmel.
C. He was taken into the heavens by a fiery chariot and horses.
D. He was poisoned by the prophets of Baal.

9. How was the general of the Syrian army cleansed of leprosy?

A. He washed seven times in the Jordan River, following Elisha's instructions.
B. He prayed to the pagan gods of Syria to be healed.
C. He offered a holocaust sacrifice to God, then covered his skin with the ashes.
D. Elisha gave him a powerful medicine that healed his skin.

10. After Elisha died, what happened when the body of a dead man happened to touch Elisha's bones in a cave?
A. Elisha's bones came back to life.
B. The bones turned instantly to dust.
C. The men who had placed the dead body there were cursed for disturbing Elisha's bones.
D. The dead man came back to life.

CHAPTER 17
The Stories of Job and Jonah

Textbook pages: 213–218
Perfect score: 100

Your Score: _____

Matching

Directions: In each blank beside a phrase, write the letter of the term that is described by that phrase. You may match more than one description to a single term. Each item is worth 4 points. 40 possible points.

A. Nineveh
B. Jonah
C. Uz
D. Satan
E. Job
F. Assyrians

_____ 1. was ridiculed by his wife for being faithful to God

_____ 2. a prophet who tried to run away from God

_____ 3. Job's accuser

_____ 4. a great city of Assyria

_____ 5. a wealthy man whose faith was severely tested

_____ 6. a wicked and brutal people who worshipped false gods

_____ 7. survived a great storm at sea

_____ 8. lost his children, servants, and animals

_____ 9. the city where Job lived

_____ 10. was covered in ulcers

Multiple Choice

Directions: For each numbered item, circle the letter beside the choice (A, B, C, or D) that best answers the question or completes the statement. Circle only one choice per item. Each correct answer is worth 6 points. 60 possible points.

1. What did God say about Job?

A. God said Job was a blameless and upright man.
B. God said Job had repented and turned from his wicked ways.
C. God said Job was a great sinner, but there was hope for him.
D. God said Job served Him only halfheartedly.

2. What claim did the Devil make about Job?

A. The Devil said that Job secretly hated God in his heart.
B. The Devil said that Job was a hypocrite.
C. The Devil said that Job loved God only because God had blessed him.
D. The Devil said that Job had broken God's commandments.

3. Why did Job suffer so many tragedies?

A. Job himself was to blame for them, because they resulted from his unwise choices.
B. Job was just in the wrong place at the wrong time.
C. God was punishing Job for his wickedness.
D. God allowed Satan to test Job.

4. What did Job do as a sign of his grief?

A. He sang sorrowful songs.
B. He tore his clothes and shaved his head.
C. He refused to eat until he nearly starved.
D. All of the above.

5. What was the final outcome of Job's trials?

A. Job remained firm in his faith, and God rewarded him.
B. Job lost faith in God's justice and died in despair.
C. Job resented God and turned away from him in rebellion.
D. Job became a priest and a prophet.

6. Why did God want Jonah to preach to the people of Nineveh?

A. They were extremely wicked, and God wanted them to repent.
B. God knew they wouldn't repent, but He wanted them to have no excuse.
C. God wanted the Assyrians to replace the Israelites as His chosen people.
D. God wanted to test Jonah's obedience.

7. Why did Jonah take a ship in the opposite direction from Nineveh?

A. He thought God was mistaken.
B. He was afraid of the cruel Assyrians.
C. He was looking for someone to take his place.
D. He wanted to take a vacation before he went on such a challenging mission.

8. When a great storm threatened to destroy the ship on which Jonah was a passenger, how was the ship's crew saved?

A. They prayed to their pagan gods, and their gods protected them.
B. They steered the ship to an island to find a safe harbor.
C. The ship broke up, but they floated to safety on pieces of the ship's debris.
D. They threw Jonah overboard, and the sea became calm.

9. How was Jonah's life preserved?

A. He prayed to God, and the sea became calm.
B. He swam to the shore of a nearby island.
C. He was rescued by sailors from a ship that passed by.
D. A great fish swallowed him and cast him up on the shore three days later.

10. How did the people of Nineveh respond to Jonah's preaching?

A. They stoned him to death as a false prophet.
B. They threw him in prison as a foreign spy.
C. They fasted, put on sackcloth, and repented of their wickedness.
D. They pretended to believe him, but they never truly repented.

PART FIVE
How God's People Went Into Exile and Returned

CHAPTER 18
The Assyrian Invasions

Textbook pages: 219–228
Perfect score: 100

Your Score: _____

Matching

Directions: In each blank beside a phrase, write the letter of the term that is described by that phrase. You may match more than one description to a single term. Each item is worth 2 points. 40 possible points.

A. Media
B. Sarah
C. Tobit
D. Amos
E. Tobias
F. Samaritans
G. Raphael

H. Hezekiah
I. Isaiah
J. Sennacherib
K. Manasseh
L. Holofernes
M. Judith

_____ 1. a Samaritan exile who kept God's commandments

_____ 2. a wicked king of Judah who went in exile to Babylon

_____ 3. the wife of Tobias

_____ 4. a great prophet who spoke to Hezekiah for God

_____ 5. one of the seven holy angels who present the prayers of the saints

_____ 6. a holy king of Judah

_____ 7. an Assyrian general

_____ 8. a land in the eastern part of Assyria

_____ 9. lost his livelihood when he became disabled

_____ 10. the son of Tobit

_____ 11. put his trust in the Egyptians instead of God

_____ 12. cut off the head of an enemy leader

_____ 13. commanded the priests and Levites to cleanse the Temple

_____ 14. a cruel and proud king of the Assyrians

_____ 15. was sent to Tobit to cure him of his illness

_____ 16. a prophet who rebuked God's people for oppressing the poor

_____ 17. exhorted his son to live a holy life

_____ 18. the stranger who served as a guide for Tobias

_____ 19. risked his life to bury the dead and help their needy relatives

_____ 20. threatened to conquer Judah's capital but was stopped by an act of God

Multiple Choice

Directions: For each numbered item, circle the letter beside the choice (A, B, C, or D) that best answers the question or completes the statement. Circle only one choice per item. Each correct answer is worth 6 points. 60 possible points.

1. When the Assyrians invaded Israel and destroyed Samaria, for what sins were the Israelites being punished?

A. idolatry and dishonesty
B. murder and adultery
C. oppression of the poor
D. all of the above

2. How did Tobit demonstrate his faith in God?

A. He obeyed the Law of Moses.
B. He performed simple acts of charity.
C. Both A and B above.
D. None of the above.

3. How did Tobit become blind?

A. He fell down a well and hit his head.
B. A serious illness left him unable to see.
C. He gradually lost his vision because of old age.
D. Bird droppings fell into his eyes.

4. How did Tobit regain his sight?

A. A prophet laid hands on him and healed him.
B. He went to the Temple to pray and was healed.
C. The gall of a fish was placed on his eyes as a salve.
D. His wife gave him a healing potion to drink.

5. Who did Tobit's guide turn out to be?

A. Raphael
B. Gabriel
C. Michael
D. his guardian angel

6. How did Hezekiah hope to keep Sennacherib from conquering Jerusalem?

A. Hezekiah offered him an enormous tribute if he would leave the country.
B. Hezekiah told him that God's wrath would consume Sennacherib's army.
C. Hezekiah offered Sennacherib generous terms of peace.
D. Hezekiah threatened to form an alliance against Sennacherib with all the neighboring peoples.

7. How was the Assyrian army prevented from capturing Jerusalem?

A. The king of Judah rallied an army of two hundred thousand men to defeat them.
B. An angel entered the Assyrian camp and killed one hundred and eighty-five thousand soldiers.
C. The army of Judah was joined by armies of their allies, the Phoenicians, the Amorites, the Moabites, and the Edomites.
D. When the Assyrian general died from a sudden illness, his army returned home.

8. Why did Judith rebuke the elders of her city, Bethulia?

A. They surrendered the city to the Assyrians.
B. They made an alliance with the Egyptians.
C. They were so busy with commerce that they ignored the Assyrian threat to the city.
D. They put God to the test by placing a time limit on His power to rescue them.

9. How did Holofernes become vulnerable to Judith's assault?

A. Judith convinced him that she wanted to help him capture her city.
B. Holofernes became drunk with wine and fell into a deep sleep.
C. Both A and B above.
D. None of the above.

10. What happened when the Assyrian army that was camped near Bethulia discovered that their leader had been killed?

A. They were so furious that they burned the city.
B. They chose a new general and marched on the city immediately.
C. They sent messengers to offer the city a peace treaty.
D. They were panic-stricken and fled to the hills, pursued by the army of Judah.

CHAPTER 19
Daniel and the Babylonian Captivity

Textbook pages: 229–242
Perfect score: 100

Your Score: _____

Matching

Directions: In each blank beside a phrase, write the letter of the term that is described by that phrase. You may match more than one description to a single term. Each item is worth 4 points. 40 possible points.

A. Belshazzar
B. Nebuchadnezzar
C. Daniel
D. Jeremiah
E. Darius
F. Habakkuk
G. Shadrach, Meshach, and Abednego
H. Ezekiel
I. Susanna
J. Medes and Persians

_____ 1. wrote the Book of Lamentations in the Bible

_____ 2. a king of Babylon who was terrified to see a mysterious hand writing on the wall

_____ 3. conquered the Babylonians

_____ 4. preserved from harm in a fiery furnace

_____ 5. falsely accused by the elders and nearly executed

_____ 6. carried by an angel to Babylon to take food to Daniel

_____ 7. Jewish prophet who encouraged his people to trust God despite their exile in Babylon

_____ 8. a king of Babylon whose dream Daniel interpreted

_____ 9. was tricked into sentencing Daniel to death

_____ 10. a prophet who interpreted dreams

Multiple Choice

Directions: For each numbered item, circle the letter beside the choice (A, B, C, or D) that best answers the question or completes the statement. Circle only one choice per item. Each correct answer is worth 6 points. 60 possible points.

1. An assembly hall where Jewish people gather to worship is called a:

A. rabbi.
B. synagogue.
C. mosque.
D. church.

2. Why did King Jehoiakim imprison Jeremiah in the mud at the bottom of a deep hole?

A. Jeremiah had publicly rebuked Jehoiakim for oppressing the poor.
B. Jeremiah had secretly instigated a rebellion against Jehoiakim.
C. Jehoiakim's wife hated Jeremiah's preaching.
D. Jeremiah had prophesied the evils that would come if Jehoiakim relied on Egypt for protection.

3. What did Jeremiah do as a warning of what was in store for the people of Jerusalem if they continued their wicked lives?

A. He walked the streets of the city with a yoke on his neck.
B. He set a bonfire ablaze in the court of the Temple.
C. He covered the marketplace with dust and ashes.
D. He slaughtered a lamb and sprinkled the blood on the walls of the king's palace.

4. Why did Jeremiah and some Levites secretly remove the Ark of the Covenant from the Temple?

A. They wanted to keep it from being destroyed when the Babylonians burned down the Temple.
B. They wanted to place it in a new Tabernacle they had built to take to Babylon in exile.
C. They wanted to march with it into battle to win a victory as their ancestors had done.
D. If Jeremiah was in possession of the Ark, he could become the new high priest.

5. How did Daniel demonstrate that Susanna's accusers were lying?

A. He had Susanna and the men draw lots so that God would show who was telling the truth.
B. He was a prophet, so he prophesied that she was innocent, and the people believed him.
C. He summoned more witnesses who contradicted their story.
D. When he questioned the two accusers separately, their stories differed.

6. What did Daniel's friends do when Nebuchadnezzar threatened to kill them if they didn't worship an idol?

A. They refused to worship the idol and praised the one true God instead.
B. They were so terrified that they obeyed immediately.
C. They bowed before the idol, but in their hearts, they still worshipped God.
D. They hid in a cave where Nebuchadnezzar's men couldn't find them.

7. If the prophet Daniel was such a holy man, why did he have enemies?

A. Babylonian officials grew jealous and angry that a Jewish man would be placed over them.
B. Daniel had demonstrated to the king that the priests of the Babylonian god Bel were frauds.
C. Both A and B above.
D. None of the above.

8. How did Daniel's enemies find a way to trap him and have him condemned to death?

A. They hid the king's golden scepter in Daniel's room and then claimed that he had stolen it.
B. They spread false rumors that he was organizing a revolt of the Jews against the king.
C. They persuaded the king to make a new law that for thirty days, no one could pray, because they knew that Daniel would not obey such a law.
D. They convinced the king's wife to falsely accuse Daniel of spying on her.

9. When Daniel was thrown into the lions' den, how was his faith rewarded?

A. The lions fell into a deep sleep and never bothered him.
B. The king secretly sent soldiers to rescue Daniel.
C. The lions weren't hungry, so they ignored Daniel.
D. God sent an angel to keep the lions from harming him.

10. What did the handwriting say that appeared mysteriously on the wall at the king's feast in Babylon?

A. It warned that the king and his guests would be punished for drinking from the sacred Temple vessels in honor of their false gods.
B. It predicted that the king would have a prosperous reign for many years to come.
C. It warned that the Jews would revolt against him and win their freedom as they did in Egypt.
D. It prophesied that the Jewish Messiah would one day come as the Savior.

CHAPTER 20
The Prophets

Textbook pages: 243–248
Perfect score: 100

Your Score: _____

Matching

Directions: In each blank beside a phrase, write the letter of the term that is described by that phrase. You may match more than one description to a single term. Each item is worth 4 points. 40 possible points.

A. Cyrus
B. Messiah
C. Immanuel
D. Isaiah
E. major prophets
F. minor prophets
G. Jeremiah
H. Ezekiel

_____ 1. a prophet who was well educated and belonged to the royal family

_____ 2. their writings fill only a few pages each in the Bible

_____ 3. known as "the Great Prophet" because of the wonderful things he foretold

_____ 4. had a vision of "four living creatures" in the midst of a cloud and fire

_____ 5. means "God with us"

_____ 6. their works take up a large part of the Old Testament

_____ 7. was left behind in the ruins of the Temple and the city of Jerusalem to mourn for his people

_____ 8. king of Persia

_____ 9. prophesied in parables, or short symbolic stories, which are sometimes hard to understand

_____ 10. the Great Deliverer whom the prophets foretold would save the world

Multiple Choice

Directions: For each numbered item, circle the letter beside the choice (A, B, C, or D) that best answers the question or completes the statement. Circle only one choice per item. Each correct answer is worth 6 points. 60 possible points.

1. Who are the four major prophets?

A. Moses, Joshua, Elijah, and Elisha
B. Isaiah, Jeremiah, Ezekiel, and Daniel
C. Ezra, Nehemiah, Tobit, and Hosea
D. Joel, Amos, Obadiah, and Jonah

2. What was the work of a prophet among the Jews?

A. He performed the ministry of a priest.
B. He foretold the future.
C. He told the people what they must do to please God at the present time.
D. Both B and C above.

3. Where did the prophets most often live?

A. apart from the people
B. in the king's palace
C. in the court of the Temple
D. in the center of Jerusalem

4. Which of the following topics is not found in Isaiah's prophecies?

A. the Exodus from Egypt
B. the coming of Christ
C. the bitter passion and death of our Savior
D. the establishment of the Church

5. For how long had Jeremiah warned the people that a terrible punishment would come upon them from God unless they repented of their sins?

A. two years
B. a month
C. forty years
D. six weeks

6. Jeremiah wrote a book that describes the destruction of Jerusalem and the great suffering of the people; this book is called:

A. Ecclesiastes.
B. Wisdom.
C. Sirach.
D. Lamentations.

7. To what audience was Ezekiel's message addressed?

A. the Jews who were left behind in Jerusalem after its destruction by the Babylonians
B. the Jews who were in captivity in Babylon
C. both A and B above
D. none of the above

8. The prophet's vision of "four living creatures" is especially significant for Christians because:

A. the vision foretells the birth of Our Lord.
B. the symbols of the four Gospel writers come from this vision.
C. the "four living creatures" represent the four cardinal virtues.
D. the vision symbolizes the final destruction of the world.

9. What faces appear on the "four living creatures"?

A. a dragon, a lion, a horse, and an eagle
B. a woman, an ox, a dove, and an eagle
C. a bear, a raven, a tiger, and an eagle
D. a man, a lion, an ox, and an eagle

10. Which of the Gospels has come to be symbolized by the face of the eagle?

A. Matthew
B. Mark
C. Luke
D. John

CHAPTER 21
The Return to Jerusalem

Textbook pages: 249–258
Perfect score: 100

Your Score: _____

Matching

Directions: In each blank beside a phrase, write the letter of the term that is described by that phrase. Each item is worth 4 points. 40 possible points.

A. Persia
B. Nehemiah
C. Zerubbabel
D. Darius
E. Esther
F. Zechariah
G. Ahasuerus
H. Haman
I. Ezra
J. Mordecai

_____ 1. one of the prophets who urged the people to continue building the Temple

_____ 2. son of Darius who searched for a queen

_____ 3. Esther's uncle

_____ 4. the Persian king's chief adviser, who plotted to overthrow him

_____ 5. the land we now call Iran

_____ 6. oversaw the rebuilding of the walls of Jerusalem

_____ 7. Jewish priest who returned to Jerusalem to restore the rites of the Temple and the religious life of the people

_____ 8. the Persian king who permitted the Jews to finish building the Temple

_____ 9. leader of the first returning exiles of Judah

_____ 10. saved the Jewish people from being massacred

Multiple Choice

Directions: For each numbered item, circle the letter beside the choice (A, B, C, or D) that best answers the question or completes the statement. Circle only one choice per item. Each correct answer is worth 6 points. 60 possible points.

1. Which of the following is *not* one of the ways in which Cyrus acted favorably toward the Jews?

A. He issued a decree that permitted all the Jews to return to the Kingdom of Judah.
B. He gave back to the Jews the sacred vessels that had been taken from the Temple by King Nebuchadnezzar.
C. He gave orders for the Temple to be rebuilt.
D. He converted to the Jewish religion and worshiped the one true God.

2. Why did many of the Jews decide to remain in Babylon when they could have returned to their homeland?

A. They were afraid to risk the dangers of a journey to Judah.
B. They had made themselves a home in Babylon, so they weren't ready to leave.
C. Both A and B above.
D. None of the above.

3. Which of the following does *not* explain why only some of the captives from the northern kingdom of Israel ever returned?

A. They had no religious leadership.
B. They had largely forgotten their native land.
C. The Assyrians, their captors, had treated them kindly and encouraged them to stay.
D. After being in captivity more than two hundred years, they had scattered to several faraway nations.

4. What did the returning Jews do as soon as they reached the city of Jerusalem?

A. They began planting crops in the fields outside the city walls so that they would have food.
B. They built an altar where they could offer sacrifices to God.
C. From the rubble of the city, they built themselves homes for their families.
D. They fortified the city walls to protect against enemies.

5. Why did some of the neighboring pagan peoples become angry with the Jews who had returned to Judah?

A. They didn't want to have neighbors of a different religion.
B. The Jews had turned down their offer to help in the rebuilding of the Temple.
C. They feared that the flocks and herds of the Jews would occupy all the pasture land.
D. They thought that the Jews planned to make war against them.

6. How long did it take to rebuild the Temple after the first cornerstone had been laid?

A. one year
B. five years
C. ten years
D. twenty years

7. Why was Esther risking her life when she approached the king and spoke to him?

A. The king was seriously ill that day and had given a command that he was not to be bothered.
B. Esther had fallen out of favor with the king, so he wanted to get rid of her and find another wife.
C. In those days, if people approached the king and spoke to him without his inviting them to do so, they could be put to death.
D. The king thought Esther was a spy, so he had been searching for her to kill her.

8. What happened to Haman after his treachery was revealed to the king?

A. He was hanged on the same gibbet that he had prepared for Mordecai.
B. He fled the palace and became a fugitive living in Judah.
C. He begged for the king's mercy and was pardoned.
D. He was imprisoned in a miserable dungeon for the rest of his life.

9. When Ezra saw that the people who had returned to Judah needed instruction in their religion, how did he provide it for them?

A. He built synagogues in the cities where the Jews lived, where they could gather and listen to the Levites read the Scriptures.
B. He sent the priests out from the Temple in Jerusalem to go teach in the cities where the Jews lived.
C. He established a Temple school in Jerusalem, where the Jews could gather from all over Judah to learn.
D. The Jews no longer spoke Hebrew, so he translated all the Scriptures into the languages they now spoke.

10. How were the Jews able to rebuild the great walls of Jerusalem in only fifty-two days?

A. The neighboring peoples of the land helped them rebuild the walls.
B. The king sent soldiers from Persia to help them rebuild the walls.
C. God gave the Jews miraculous strength so they could work twenty-four hours a day without stopping until the job was done.
D. Every Jewish family was assigned a certain section of the walls to rebuild.

CHAPTER 22
The Last Days of the Kingdom of Judah

Textbook pages: 259–271
Perfect score: 100

Your Score: _____

Matching

Directions: In each blank beside a phrase, write the letter of the term that is described by that phrase. Each item is worth 4 points. 40 possible points.

A. Alexander the Great
B. Heliodorus
C. Judea
D. Eleazar
E. Seleucus IV
F. Maccabees
G. Onias
H. Judas
I. Antiochus Epiphanes
J. Antiochus Eupator

_____ 1. one of the successors of Alexander the Great whose portion of the empire included Palestine

_____ 2. entered the Temple, removed the sacred vessels, plundered the treasury, and offered unclean animals on the altar

_____ 3. succeeded his father as commander of the Maccabees

_____ 4. king of Syria during the time of the Maccabees

_____ 5. what the land of Judah came to be called

_____ 6. a high priest in Jerusalem who hated evil

_____ 7. king of the Greek kingdom of Macedon

_____ 8. an officer of Seleucus who demanded the funds from the Temple treasury

_____ 9. an elderly Jew who was scourged and beaten to death for refusing to eat pork

_____ 10. leaders of a Jewish revolt against the Greeks

Multiple Choice

Directions: For each numbered item, circle the letter beside the choice (A, B, C, or D) that best answers the question or completes the statement. Circle only one choice per item. Each correct answer is worth 6 points. 60 possible points.

1. What three continents did the great Persian Empire span?

A. Asia, Africa, and Egypt
B. Europe, Asia, and Africa
C. Africa, Europe, and Greece
D. India, Africa, and Asia

2. Just as the Assyrian Empire was conquered by the Babylonians, and the Babylonian Empire was conquered by the Persians, the Persian Empire was conquered by:

A. the Greeks under Alexander.
B. the Romans under Caesar.
C. the Egyptians under Pharaoh.
D. None of the above.

3. What happened to the officer sent by Seleucus to demand the funds from the Temple treasury?

A. He took the treasure, but he fled to Egypt with it so he could keep it for himself.
B. He took the treasure, but he died of a sudden illness on the way back to Seleucus.
C. God blinded him so that he couldn't find the treasure.
D. He was scourged by heavenly messengers who kept him from seizing the treasure.

4. How did Antiochus Epiphanes try to force the Jews to worship the gods of the Greeks?

A. The Temple of the true God was made the temple of false gods so that pagans went there to worship their idols.
B. In all the cities of Judah, pagan altars were set up and pagan worship was required.
C. Anyone who followed the laws of the Jews and who observed the Sabbath was punished by death.
D. All of the above.

5. Why did Eleazar refuse even to pretend he was eating pork in order to escape death at the hands of the Greeks?

A. He knew that God would perform a miracle to keep him from feeling any pain.
B. He knew that even if men can deceive their kings, they cannot deceive God.
C. He was an elderly man and knew he would soon be dying anyway.
D. All of the above.

6. Once the Jews led by the Maccabees were victorious over Antiochus and gained peace, what changes did they make in Jerusalem?

question continued on next page ➡

A. They purified the Temple, which had been used for pagan sacrifices, and consecrated a new altar of sacrifice.

B. They rebuilt the royal palace of David so Judas could live in it as king.

C. They built a new and better wall around the city to protect it from their enemies.

D. They dug new tunnels to bring water from deep springs into the city, so that their enemies couldn't cut off their water supply.

7. How did Judas react when he discovered that some of his soldiers killed in battle had carried a token of pagan idols, which God had forbidden?

A. He tore his clothes, covered himself with dust and ashes, and wept aloud because he knew that God's wrath would condemn the soldiers on judgment day.

B. In anger, he left the bodies of the soldiers unburied so that the vultures would eat them.

C. He sent the pagan idols home to the soldiers' families as a token of respect for their religion.

D. He ordered a large sum of money to be sent to Jerusalem to be used for a sacrifice, with prayers, to be offered for the sins of the dead soldiers.

8. What gave Judas the confidence to go to battle against the Syrians commanded by Nicanor, even though the Jewish forces were greatly outnumbered?

A. Judas had a vision in which the high priest Onias and the prophet Jeremiah appeared to him and promised victory.

B. God opened the eyes of Judas to see angels marching to war alongside the Jewish troops.

C. Judas's wife had a dream in which Nicanor was killed and the Syrian troops fled.

D. Jewish spies returned from the Syrian camp with assurances that the enemy troops were poorly trained and equipped.

9. How did the Jews finally find a way to protect themselves against the Syrians?

A. The Jews fortified their cities so thoroughly that the Syrians couldn't capture them.

B. The Jews made an alliance with Rome, in which the Romans promised to protect the Jews.

C. The Jews raised a joint army with the Ammonites, Edomites, and Moabites that was able to defend all of the region against Syria.

D. The Maccabees launched a surprise attack against Damascus that caused the Syrian troops to be called back home.

10. How did the Roman emperor end the civil wars and restore order in Judea right after the period of Maccabean rule?

A. He sent Roman troops to crush the armies on both sides of the civil wars.

B. He sent an ambassador to help the Jewish factions agree to a peace treaty.

C. He appointed an Edomite named Herod to become the new king.

D. He exiled the Jews from Judea once more and replaced them with exiles from other nations.

Answer Key

INTRODUCTION – Your Time Has Come
Test Book pages 9–12

Multiple Choice
1. D   2. C   3. D.   4. A   5. C   6. B   7. B   8. D   9. D   10. A   11. B   12. B
13. D   14. C   15. A

Old Testament or New?
1. NT	2. NT	3. OT	4. NT	5. OT	6. NT
7. OT	8. OT	9. OT	10. OT	11. OT	12. OT
13. NT	14. NT	15. NT	16. OT	17. OT	18. NT
19. OT	20. OT				

PART ONE – How God Came to Promise Us a Redeemer

CHAPTER 1 – In the Beginning
Test Book pages 13–16

True or False?
1. F   2. T   3. T   4. F   5. F   6. T   7. T   8. T   9. F   10. F

Matching
1. D   2. F   3. G   4. A   5. E   6. C   7. B

Multiple Choice
1. B   2. D   3. C   4. D   5. A   6. B   7. A   8. C   9. C   10. C   11. D   12. A
13. C   14. B

CHAPTER 2 – The Descendants of Adam and Eve
Test Book pages 17–20

Matching
1. G   2. H   3. A   4. A   5. C   6. F   7. D   8. A   9. B   10. E   11. A   12. D
13. E   14. A   15. C   16. E   17. A   18. D   19. H   20. H

Multiple Choice
1. C   2. D   3. B   4. A   5. D   6. C   7. A   8. A   9. D   10. A

PART TWO – How God Founded the Nation From Which the Redeemer of the World Came

CHAPTER 3 – Abraham and Isaac
Test Book pages 21–24

Matching
1. E   2. G   3. F   4. D   5. B   6. L   7. F   8. A   9. C   10. I   11. H   12. M
13. A   14. B   15. A   16. A   17. K   18. A   19. J   20. F

Multiple Choice
1. B   2. D   3. A   4. D   5. D   6. C   7. B   8. A   9. D   10. C

CHAPTER 4 – Jacob, the Son of Isaac
Test Book pages 25–28

Matching
1. E   2. A   3. B   4. H   5. A   6. J   7. K   8. A   9. I   10. A   11. C   12. B
13. B   14. A   15. F   16. A   17. G   18. A   19. B   20. D

Multiple Choice
1. D   2. C   3. D   4. B   5. D   6. A   7. D   8. A   9. D   10. C

CHAPTER 5 – Joseph, the Son of Jacob
Test Book pages 29–32

Matching
1. C   2. H   3. A   4. J   5. G   6. K   7. K   8. K   9. A   10. D   11. A   12. I
13. L   14. A   15. F   16. C   17. M   18. A   19. A   20. E

Multiple Choice
1. D   2. B   3. A   4. D   5. B   6. C   7. D   8. C   9. B   10. A

PART THREE – How God Protected His Chosen People and Led Them Into the Promised Land

CHAPTER 6 – God Calls Moses to Lead His People
Test Book pages 33–36

Matching

1. H   2. I   3. A   4. D   5. F   6. G   7. B   8. C   9. B   10. F   11. B   12. E

Name the Plagues

In order:

1. waters turned to blood
2. frogs
3. gnats
4. flies
5. animals (livestock) died
6. boils
7. hail
8. locusts
9. darkness

Multiple Choice

1. D   2. D   3. D   4. A   5. B   6. C   7. C   8. C   9. A   10. B

CHAPTER 7 – The Escape From Egypt
Test Book pages 37–40

Matching

1. B   2. I   3. J   4. D   5. C   6. E   7. A   8. G   9. F   10. H

Multiple Choice

1. B   2. A   3. D   4. A   5. C   6. B   7. C   8. B   9. A   10. D

CHAPTER 8 – The Revelation of God's Law
Test Book pages 41–44

Matching

1. C   2. T   3. F   4. P   5. Y   6. U   7. S   8. W   9. N   10. A   11. K   12. O
13. M   14. J   15. D   16. E   17. I   18. L   19. R   20. G   21. V   22. X   23. B   24. H
25. Q

Multiple Choice

1. D   2. D   3. A   4. B   5. C   6. C   7. D   8. B   9. A   10. C

CHAPTER 9 – The Desert Wanderings of the Israelites
Test Book pages 45–48

Matching
1. J   2. E   3. H   4. I   5. G   6. D   7. F   8. A   9. C   10. B

Multiple Choice
1. B   2. C   3. C   4. A   5. C   6. B   7. A   8. D   9. C   10. D

CHAPTER 10 – Joshua, Commander of the Israelites
Test Book pages 49–52

Matching
1. E   2. G   3. C   4. I   5. F   6. J   7. A   8. D   9. H   10. B

Multiple Choice
1. B   2. C   3. D   4. B   5. A   6. D   7. C   8. C   9. D   10. A

CHAPTER 11 – The Israelites in the Promised Land
Test Book pages 53–56

Matching
1. B   2. J   3. G   4. H   5. F   6. I   7. D   8. C   9. E   10. A

Multiple Choice
1. C   2. A   3. B   4. C   5. D   6. B   7. D   8. A   9. D   10. C

PART FOUR – How God's Chosen People Lived Under Their Kings

CHAPTER 12 – Saul and David
Test Book pages 57–60

Matching
1. F   2. G   3. E   4. B   5. H   6. A   7. D   8. I   9. C   10. G

Multiple Choice
1. D   2. D   3. A   4. C   5. D   6. C   7. B   8. C   9. A   10. C

CHAPTER 13 – David's Reign
Test Book pages 61-64

Matching
1. C   2. F   3. D   4. I   5. A   6. H   7. B   8. E   9. B   10. G

Multiple Choice
1. B   2. A   3. B   4. A   5. C   6. C   7. A   8. D   9. B   10. D

CHAPTER 14 – The Israelites Under King Solomon
Test Book pages 65-68

Matching
1. D   2. E   3. A   4. M   5. J   6. G   7. A   8. G   9. B   10. A   11. A   12. N
13. A   14. K   15. C   16. I   17. H   18. O   19. F   20. L

Multiple Choice
1. B   2. D   3. A.   4. D   5. D   6. B   7. C   8. D   9. D   10. A

CHAPTER 15 – Jeroboam and Rehoboam
Test Book pages 69-72

Matching
1. E   2. A   3. H   4. C   5. B   6. F   7. G   8. B   9. D   10. B

Multiple Choice
1. B   2. A   3. D   4. C   5. C   6. B   7. C   8. D   9. B   10. B

CHAPTER 16 – Elijah the Prophet
Test Book pages 73-76

Matching
1. E   2. G   3. F   4. J   5. H   6. I   7. D   8. A   9. B   10. C

Multiple Choice
1. B   2. A   3. D   4. B   5. C   6. A   7. D   8. C   9. A   10. D

CHAPTER 17 – The Stories of Job and Jonah
Test Book pages 77–80

Matching
1. E   2. B   3. D   4. A   5. E   6. F   7. B   8. E   9. C   10. E

Multiple Choice
1. A   2. C   3. D   4. B   5. A   6. A   7. B   8. D   9. D   10. C

PART FIVE – How God's People Went Into Exile and Returned

CHAPTER 18 – The Assyrian Invasions
Test Book pages 81–84

Matching
1. E   2. K   3. B   4. I   5. G   6. H   7. L   8. A   9. C   10. E   11. H   12. M
13. H   14. J   15. G   16. D   17. C   18. G   19. C   20. J

Multiple Choice
1. D   2. C   3. D   4. C   5. A   6. A   7. B   8. D   9. C   10. D

CHAPTER 19 – Daniel and the Babylonian Captivity
Test Book pages 85–88

Matching
1. D   2. A   3. J   4. G   5. I   6. F   7. H   8. B   9. E   10. C

Multiple Choice
1. B   2. D   3. A   4. A   5. D   6. A   7. C   8. C   9. D   10. A

CHAPTER 20 – The Prophets
Test Book pages 89–92

Matching
1. D   2. F   3. D   4. H   5. C   6. E   7. G   8. A   9. H   10. B

Multiple Choice
1. B   2. D   3. A   4. A   5. C   6. D   7. C   8. B   9. D   10. D

CHAPTER 21 – The Return to Jerusalem
Test Book pages 93-96

Matching
1. F   2. G   3. J   4. H   5. A   6. B   7. I   8. D   9. C   10. E

Multiple Choice
1. D   2. C   3. C   4. B   5. B   6. D   7. C   8. A   9. A   10. D

CHAPTER 22 – The Last Days of the Kingdom of Judah
Test Book pages 97-100

Matching
1. E   2. I   3. H   4. J   5. C   6. G   7. A   8. B   9. D   10. F

Multiple Choice
1. B   2. A   3. D   4. D   5. B   6. A   7. D   8. A   9. B   10. C

 TAN·BOOKS

TAN Books was founded in 1967 to preserve the spiritual, intellectual and liturgical traditions of the Catholic Church. At a critical moment in history TAN kept alive the great classics of the Faith and drew many to the Church. In 2008 TAN was acquired by Saint Benedict Press. Today TAN continues its mission to a new generation of readers.

From its earliest days TAN has published a range of booklets that teach and defend the Faith. Through partnerships with organizations, apostolates, and mission-minded individuals, well over 10 million TAN booklets have been distributed.

More recently, TAN has expanded its publishing with the launch of Catholic calendars and daily planners—as well as Bibles, fiction, and multimedia products through its sister imprints Catholic Courses (CatholicCourses.com) and Saint Benedict Press (SaintBenedictPress.com). In 2015, TAN Homeschool became the latest addition to the TAN family, preserving the Faith for the next generation of Catholics (www.TANHomeschool.com).

Today TAN publishes over 500 titles in the areas of theology, prayer, devotions, doctrine, Church history, and the lives of the saints. TAN books are published in multiple languages and found throughout the world in schools, parishes, bookstores and homes.

For a free catalog, visit us online at
TANBooks.com

Or call us toll-free at
(800) 437-5876